Critical acclaim for I
memoir of life

GRAND CENTRAL WINTER

A *New York Times* Notable Book of the Year

"The prose lengthens out into easy strides, the story-telling is sound and the characters fresh. . . ."
— *The New York Times Book Review*

"Stringer's crisp detail, straight no-chaser wit, and uncompromising frankness are as bracing as his subject is significant."
— *Booklist*

"[A] candid, sad, yet upbeat memoir. . . . Stringer possesses a sharp eye for the street and the rich, sagacious talent of a storyteller."
— *Publishers Weekly*

"The book gives full humanity to its troubled characters and homes in on the motivations, strategies, and relationships of people surviving on the streets. . . . Highly recommended."
— *Library Journal*

"Stringer weaves his gritty scenes with fluid commentary on how things work and what they mean, in language that combines the punch of the streets with the ideas of a careful thinker."
— New York *Daily News*

GRAND CENTRAL WINTER

STORIES FROM THE STREET

LEE STRINGER

WASHINGTON SQUARE PRESS
PUBLISHED BY POCKET BOOKS

New York   London   Toronto   Sydney   Singapore

WSP A Washington Square Press Publication of
POCKET BOOKS, a division of Simon & Schuster Inc.
1230 Avenue of the Americas, New York, NY 10020

Copyright © 1998 by Caverly Stringer
Afterword copyright © 1999 by Caverly Stringer

Published by arrangement with Seven Stories Press

ISBN: 0-671-03654-8

First Washington Square Press trade paperback printing November 1999

10 9 8 7 6 5 4 3 2 1

WASHINGTON SQUARE PRESS and colophon are registered trademarks of Simon & Schuster Inc.

Cover design by Brigid Pearson
Front cover photos by Cheung Ching Ming

Printed in the U.S.A.

Contents

His name is Lee Stringer. Like Jack London, he is a self-educated storyteller of the first rank, and an unembittered, hopeful survivor of extreme poverty, long-term homelessness, and addiction.

Lee Stringer's tales are grimly entertaining. They are about how the most useless and rootless and endlessly harried of New York City's outcasts manage to stay alive day after day. They are reportage, not fiction. The author, himself a character in every story, was for years and years as bereft of dignity and self-respect as are his subjects.

Even when a crack addict, though, gathering cans redeemable for a nickle apiece, being chased off subways for hawking *Street News*, a weekly about and by pariahs like himself, Lee Stringer discovered a new high. It was writing for that paper. He wrote so interestingly and well that he became editor. He gained a purpose in life beyond getting the next crack fix. On the paper's office couch, he at least found a place to sleep where police could not improve the quality of life in the city by rousting him.

He kicked his drug habit. That makes him worthy of our attention, however fleeting, as a small-time hero. But this man can write! His stories are deliberately unsentimental. He might have made himself and his wretched characters from real life seem lovable or cute or raffish, or at least pitiable, and thus established himself as a sort of Damon Runyon.

He chooses instead to be coolly technical, to teach his readers what homeless persons in New York City, many of them clinically insane or idiotic, do hour-after-hour, day-after-day, simply to keep from dying.

Nowhere in all his first-rate writing has Lee Stringer concealed the hook of collective guilt, should we dare to bite. But those who do bite will find resonant new dimensions, as have I.

What is to be done?

—Kurt Vonnegut
New York City
May 13, 1998

In some eras more than others it is harder for us all to be the kind of people we would wish ourselves to be. This was certainly true of Germany in the forties. And to an extent it was also true of America in the eighties, as the mighty and the lowly alike went to extraordinary lengths to flee a deepening sense of despair. The grand exploits of the high-and-mightiest—headlining the news as they had—were well documented and since have been amply dissected. But for the low and the lost, less is understood about their sprees of abandon.

I was one among them.

This, in part, is our story.

Acknowledgments

I can hardly pick up a Seven Stories Press book without finding unbridled praise for publisher Dan Simon at the top of its acknowledgments. And much as I like to buck a trend, I find myself hastening to join that pack. There's no getting around the fact that Dan is indeed a gem. Were it not for his guidance I would have committed wholesale blunder to print.

He has my marker.

I owe a debt of gratitude as well to the erstwhile Nelson Algren, who told me, posthumously, that writers are at their best when they don't know what they are doing.

Thank you, Mr. Algren. For me there has been no greater manic-depressive lunacy than the process of trying to write this book. From prophet to fraud, from exhilaration to cold sweat, I had no idea of how I was going to get away with it. But Nelson, peering over my shoulder from the grave, kept coaxing me on.

"Fuck all that and write," he said.

Also Janet Wickenhaver-Allon, my former *Street News* editor, who told me, "Stick to telling stories and you'll be okay"; Peter Blauner, who took precious time out from writing best-sellers to help me through a lot of angst; George McDonald, who, after working with street people for over fifteen years, still sees human beings when he looks at them; and Barbara Dunne, who not only forgave the time I betrayed her trust, but even corrected my many typos.

Among the must-mentions I include the earnest people of Project Renewal, who coaxed me back to sanity; the customer-friendly folks at the Little Computer Store, who treated me—and my oft-ailing Mac—as if I were a budding Hemingway; Jon Hart, Barbara Bales, Pat, and Indio at *Street News;* my very patient mother; and all the people, places, and things that lie at the heart of this book.

L.S.
Mamaroneck, N.Y.
March 1998

1

What happened was I was digging around in my hole—there's this long, narrow, crawl space in Grand Central's lower regions, of which few people are aware and into which I moved some time ago. It is strung with lights and there is a water spigot just outside the cubbyhole through which I enter. It's on the chilly side in winter, and I baste down there in summer, but it is, as they say, home.

I have filled this place with blankets and books and have fortified it with enough cardboard baffles to hold any rats at bay (the secret being, of course, to never bring food down here. It's the food that attracts them). So, at the end of the day I come down here to polish off that last, lonely blast. Or just to sleep it off.

But as I said, I was digging around in this hole—lying flat on my back, reaching back and under the old blankets, newspapers, and clothes that I've amassed over time and that keep me insulated from the concrete floor, trying to find some small, dowellike instrument with which to push the screens from one end of my stem to the other, so that I could smoke the remaining resin caked up in the thing.

For those of you who have not had the pleasure, I point out that when you are piping up, the first thing to go is your patience.

And I'm digging around under this mess, cursing and muttering under my breath like an old wino on a three-day drunk, when my fingers finally wrap around some sort of smooth, straight stick.

I pull it out and it's a pencil and it does the trick. I push my screens and take a hit and have a pleasurable half hour of sweaty, trembling panic that at any second someone or something is going to jump out of the darkness—I get much too paranoid to smoke with the lights on—and stomp the living shit out of me or something.

That's the great thing about being a veteran crackhead.

Always a lot of fun.

Anyway, the point is, I start carrying this pencil around with me because I really hate like hell to be caught without something to push with and then have to go searching or digging around like I was doing when I found the thing.

The good thing about carrying a pencil is that it's a pencil. And if I get stopped and searched for any reason, it's just a pencil. Of course I carry my stem around too. And there's no doubt about what that's for. But, hey, I'm not looking to strain my cerebral cortex on the subject. It's all I can do just to hustle up enough scratch every day and go cop something decent—without getting beat, arrested, or shot—so I can have a lovely time cowering in the dark for a couple of hours.

So I have this pencil with me all the time and then one day I'm sitting there in my hole with nothing to smoke and nothing to do and I pull the pencil out just to look at the film of residue stuck to the sides—you do that sort of thing when you don't have any shit—and it dawns on me that it's a pencil. I mean it's got a lead in it and all, and you can write with the thing.

So now I'm at it again. Digging around in my hole. Because I know there's an old composition book down there somewhere and I figure maybe I can distract myself for a little while by writing something.

The things a person will do when he's not smoking.

The funny thing is, I get into it.

I mean really get into it.

I start off just writing about a friend of mine. Just describing his cluttered apartment. How I kind of like the clutter. How it gives the place a lived-in look. How you can just about read his life by looking around.

So I'm writing away, and the more I write, the easier it gets. And the easier it gets, the better the writing gets, until it's like I'm just taking dictation.

Pretty soon I forget all about hustling and getting a hit. I'm scribbling like a maniac; heart pumping, adrenaline rushing, hands trembling. I'm so excited I almost crap on myself.

It's just like taking a hit.

Before I know it, I have a whole story.

I go to read the thing and it's a mess. The pages are all out of order. Parts are scratched out. Other parts are written sideways in the margins. But what I can read looks pretty good.

Even great in parts.

By the time I go back and carefully rewrite the thing, it's too late at night for me to bother going out, which is a remarkable thing for me because I don't think there's been a day since I started that I have gone without at least one hit.

So I read the story over and over.

Fix a few things.

And what I end up with reads like Tennessee Williams (I have a paperback with all his short stories in it) in the way it kind of comes in through the side door. I mean, Williams will start off talking about, say, what it smells like to work in a shoe factory and before you know it, he's going on about wanting to kill his father or something like that.

That's how my story went.

It started with my friend's house and then I have a guy sitting there with him who wants to get some pills from him so he can take himself out before the AIDS virus gets him—you see, he is HIV positive—and when he gets the pills, he goes over to the park to just lie down and fade away on the grass.

Only he feels the need to apologize to the world because he has to die in public. And someone will have to come along and pick up his sorry, dead ass and all. But he's homeless, there's no place for him to go.

I guess they'll never make a musical out of it.

But the thing is—and this is what gets me—when I read the story, I can feel this guy's pain! I mean, I haven't been able to feel much of anything in years. And there I am, sitting down there under Grand Central, reading this thing scribbled in an old composition book, and I'm practically in tears.

The next day I take the story over to my friend's house and he reads it. All I'm expecting from him is a sarcastic remark because this guy is one of those snob alcoholics. He doesn't approve of anything. Ever.

Least of all me.

But he just puts it down quietly when he finishes and gives me the slightest nod. Then he says,

"*Do* you love me?"

I know why he asks this.

Because in the story the two guys are friends but they would never admit it. They just hang around together putting each other down all the time—a lot like my friend and me—and in the end the one guy is sorry because he'll never have the chance to tell his buddy that he loves him—in a normal sort of way, I mean—and that he'll miss him.

He never realizes this until he's dying.

The only real difference between the story and me and my friend, come to think of it, is that I'm not HIV-positive and I'm not dying.

But my friend is.

And when he asks me whether or not I love him, it gets to me because I would never have thought he gave a shit one way or the other. So I go over to him and hug him, and that weepy shit starts kicking up again.

What can I tell you?

It was one of those moments.

All because I sat in my hole and wrote this little story.

Next thing you know, I'm up at the *Street News* office with it, asking if anybody'd be interested in putting it in the paper, and—sure enough—damned if I don't open up the next issue and there's my story!

That's how I got my first thing published in *Street News.*

I think I called it "No Place to Call Home."

A couple of months later I had a regular column in there. And—one thing after the other—I had the writing bug.

After that there were *four* things I did every day. Hustle up money, cop some stuff, beam up, and write. And in the end I wound up dropping the other three.

2

When I was out there, it occurred to a great many people to ask what a guy like me was doing on the street. After all, I had the full use of all my limbs, and I didn't appear to have any particular mental deficiencies. So, what, these people wanted to know, had happened?

I see it somewhat like a play, in three succinct acts.

Act I. East Side, Fall, 1984. *It is going on one o'clock on a Sunday afternoon when I exit the Lexington Avenue subway station at Thirty-third Street. The streets are awash with a bleak, gray light, which does nothing for my sour disposition. But at least the bracing September air keeps me from puking. My hangover has been at me ever since I reluctantly dragged myself out of bed.*

The phone tried to summon me three times.

Seven, eight rings each time.

But I knew what would happen if I let in the light of day. The room would begin to float, my head would begin to pound, my teeth would begin to itch....

I held on to sleep for as long as I could.

The phone be damned.

I am now on my way to Bellevue Hospital. I have a vague recollection of where it is. In one of its wings lies the city morgue. I know this because I have been there once before, in the dead of spring, to identify the corpse of my business partner, Barry. He stepped out the door one evening and his heart attacked him. The day after Easter two detectives came to the door.

"Do you know this man?" they wanted to know, and showed me the grim Polaroid. A death face. Eyes and mouth wide with surprise. Spooked by the reaper.

A wind has kicked up.

Swirls of litter dance at my feet as Bellevue's grimy brick facade looms up ahead of me. I am struck by how closely it resembles a prison. A short, gray-haired man walks solemnly toward me as I descend the entrance ramp. His head is swathed in bandages and his arm hangs in a sling. I imagine that I know what his Saturday night was about. I see rum, rancor, and rude contention. The scene plays vividly in my head.

I walk though the glass doors with this sudden prescience—almost an out-of-body experience. I can see not only the faces and bodies of the people milling through the veneered lobby but their lives as well. Each conveys to me some sense of where they live, what pictures are on their walls, who is beside them when they turn over in bed.

I find the starched, white efficiency of the nurse behind the reception desk intolerable for some reason. I survey her for a chink in her armor. A smudge, a wrinkle, a stray hair; something to connect her to humanity. But she seems seamless.

For a second I try imagining her in the throes of passion. Her hair splashed wildly against a pillow, her white, stockinged legs above her head. Moaning and growling in animal abandon with each blunt thrust. But the smile she puts on for me is all professional, conveying nothing more than—

"—Yes?"

"Visitor's pass for Wayne Stringer," I say, as curt and clipped as she. Her thumb wanders through the index cards in front of her.

"One minute," she chirps, still looking.

But I discover that I know what she is about to tell me; that in fact I knew it even before I woke up. The minute the phone had started ringing for the third time.

"Are you related to the patient?" she wants to know.

"I'm his brother," I tell her.

"I'm sorry," she says. "Haven't you been notified? I'm afraid Mr. Stringer died late last night."

There is no shock or surprise. Just a strange, rehearsed raggedness to the moment. I am a director, and she has delivered her lines exactly right.

Cut!

How characteristic of Wayne to make himself larger in absence than he was when present. To express displeasure, he often put on his disappearing act. Cross a certain line with him and ZAP! You'd be left confronting an impenetrable void, with little to do but wonder what you'd done wrong. In a family like ours, which shared loneliness like

hand-me-down clothing, my brother's slow-burning pout was a particularly potent weapon.

And I was particularly vulnerable to it. I may have thought I
had little use for Wayne most of the time, but when he'd cut me off
like that, nothing in this world mattered as much as getting back on
his good side. Usually I would resort to some verbal antics. For I was
one of the very few people who could, when I put my mind to it,
catch the abstract and slightly macabre rhythm of Wayne's sense of
humor and make him laugh.

But Wayne could be one stubborn son of a bitch. When he did-
n't want to laugh, nothing on this earth could make him so much as
crack a grin. Lord knows I never had anything near his resolve. And
Lord knows how desperately I mined for the nuggets of his laughter.

Mostly Wayne disappeared into his piano. He would sit for
hours, oblivious to the world, languidly picking at the keys. It got so
you could travel the landscape of his shifting temperament by listening to the impromptu dance his fingers performed on the keyboard.
They would twitch discordantly on the sharps and flats when he was
annoyed, making the whole room ring with his impatience. When
he was bored, they would meander the scales, aimless and atonal, off
to nowhere in particular. And when they stalked the minor chords,
somber and funereal, you could measure the depth of his glumness.

"Wayne lacked confidence," my mother would say, trying to make
sense of the fact that he never made a profession of his music. My take

on it was that what went on between Wayne and his piano was too personal for him to offer up for public consumption.

Although I was a year younger than Wayne, I was the first to leave home. A year or two after graduating high school I was gone, off in a rush. But Wayne was in no rush. He had taken a job at a hardware store down the street, and seemed perfectly content to remain where he was, buttoned down, bottled up, a shade too sober and conservative for his years.

When I returned home about two years later, having conquered considerably less of the world than I had imagined I would, I found that in the intervening time Wayne had started acting a lot more like me. At least as it concerned my less-than-wholesome facets.

He had gleefully interred his former icons—Messrs. Bach, Mozart, Beethoven, Schubert, Tchaikovsky, and company—beneath a deluge of freshly minted rock and pop recordings—some six hundred of them. Sitting with Wayne in his room the day of my return, amid the whirlybird din of a Pink Floyd opus, as he juggled a joint, a cigarette, and a beer all at the same time, I should have seen the love in his overt bid for my approval. But what I felt was a terrible sadness. For even though I may have written him off as a fuddy-duddy and a square, the truth was I had always loved, admired and greatly respected Wayne as he was. And it unnerved me to bear witness to the rude influence I had had upon him.

Such was the persistent irony between us. Both of us routinely missing the obvious, always hovering just shy of real kinship, even while we each campaigned to win the other over. It was Wayne who finally openly took the initiative. And he did it just scant months before I would be faced once again, but this time irreversibly, with his absence.

I was still reeling from my partner's sudden demise, and the legal melee that resulted from it, when Wayne appeared at my door, thirty-four years old, penniless, pale, dangerously thin, a bewildered look on his face, black-and-blue blotches all over his legs. I told myself he had bruised himself somehow and I set him up on the living room couch, thinking, *This will soon blow over and then I will be free of this bother.*

But he could barely eat. And he tossed and turned the nights away. I dragged him to a high-rent doctor. He checked him over, but had nothing to offer but a grim, confounded shrug. When I could no longer bear seeing Wayne writhe in pain on the couch, I appealed to an acquaintance of mine, who forged prescriptions. But neither painkillers nor sleeping pills had much effect. Wayne just lay there, day after day, taking his agony as he did most everything else, in frightened silence.

I seem to remember starting to feel like something was chasing me. I hid from it during the day in my work. And there was no shortage of that, or of problems to go with it. My business partner and I had been sharing our two-bedroom, rent-stabilized apartment, which doubled as our office. But his name was on the eighteen-year-old lease. And the landlord couldn't wait to dump me so that he could enjoy full Upper West Side market value for the space. Barry's son—and executor of what there was of his estate—came sniffing around to see if there was any money to be wrung out of our graphic design company. I was about ready to pull in my shingle altogether and had been offered a job with a small consumer products company. That took care of the days. Nights I went out and drank myself numb.

One night I came fumbling through the door, head swimming with booze, to find Wayne, standing in the middle of the darkened living room, a near skeleton in dirty, drooping drawers. And it broke the spell of my denial. There was no more avoiding how very sick he was. And I realized that the thing that had been chasing me was a sense of guilt.

"I was waiting here to tell you," he said softly and sadly. "That I know you were always for me, I know you were always on my side."

I couldn't say anything. Just stood there blinking into the darkness as Wayne teetered over to me and kissed me, cracked, chalky lips and all.

I took him to Bellevue Hospital first thing the next day and stayed with him until someone would see him. Eight hours in the waiting room, Wayne squirming beside me all the while. But once they discovered he was unemployed and uninsured, they didn't want his bother any more than I had. And so long as it was apparent that Wayne could make it back out the door on his own two feet, they refused to admit him.

But I shamed them into it.

"I SUPPOSE YOU'LL BE HAPPY TO TAKE HIM WHEN HE'S DOA!" I roared at the top of my lungs. The whole floor came to a stop. They were left with no choice but to take him in.

It turned out Bellevue didn't have any solutions to offer either. They weren't even sure what the hell it was Wayne had. First they said vasculitis, then they said AIDS. One day I arrived to visit him and it's all about gloves and masks and quarantine, and the next time I come, all the precautions are off. He got a little better, then he got worse, and then he was dead.

Everybody has their share of bad news to swallow. But the thing with my brother caught me off guard. So long as he had been around, I was content to pretend I didn't give a rat's ass about him. But once he was gone, the jig was up on that game.

I was able to keep up my happy-camper act for almost two years after that. I immersed myself in my new job, and found myself an apartment.

Whatever money didn't go to rent I poured into diversion.

Then one night in my apartment, alone with a bottle of Georgi's, I found myself going ten rounds with a rolled-up carpet I had leaning against the wall. I laid into the thing, roundhouse swings, all my weight behind each one. But all it got me was bleeding knuckles. For there I was again after all, doing the thing I wanted to be done with, sitting on the floor, bawling into my sleeve.

Act II. Two Days Later. *I'm knocking back doubles in some over-priced East Side bar. Eight hours and still I can't shake the feeling that I want to smash something. But by two a.m. I'm too blitzed to start any real trouble. There's nothing left for me but to go home and sleep it off.*

Lucky for me my twenty-something bar buddy, Ed from New Jersey, has his Chevy and offers to drop me off. He deposits me at my apartment door and wheels back off into the night. I make a wobbly beeline for the bed, shedding clothing as I go.

I'm dead out when my door buzzer sounds. It's one of those annoying, tinny-voiced jobs that let out a shrill, petulant squeal that can't be ignored. It doesn't summon me so much as piss me off. For some reason I'm compelled to gather my discarded clothes from the floor as I make for the door.

I'm clutching them as I let Ed in.

"How're you feeling?" he wants to know.

"Like shit," I tell him.

"I've got something that will definitely make it better." He grins.

"Come on with it," I tell him.

He halts a few paces inside the door and requests a saucer and razor. But I'm already back on the bed, my body just waiting to extract swirling, nauseating revenge if I push the up-and-about act another second.

"Saucer's in the cabinet over your head," I tell him. "Razor's in the bathroom."

A little bustle and clatter and he has them.

He removes a small wad of tin foil from his pocket and unwraps a lima-bean-size nugget the color of cream. It makes a surprisingly sharp click when he drops it on the dish. A substantial sound. One that will forever after divide two different points in time in my life.

From the bed I watch Ed at work, bent over the counter, a chef whipping up some special delicacy. I'm transfixed. He carefully and precisely halves the rock, produces a Pyrex pipe—one with a bowl, not unlike those I once smoked hash in—drops a chunk into it, and walks over to me, pipe in one hand, lighter in the other.

"Age before beauty," he says.

I am no stranger to cocaine. It has fueled my after-hours wanderings on more than one occasion—and without morning-after agonies. A blessing, as far as I am concerned.

I have never smoked it before.

But what the hell.

"Pearls before swine," I retort.

I draw on the stem, and the bowl fills with a thick, swirling cloud. I cannot feel the heat of the smoke as it goes down. But I can taste it. It is a taste I know I am going to love. The taste of success, love, orgasm, omnipotence, immortality, and winning the lottery all rolled into one.

And then some.

My hangover evaporates like steam off a griddle. The dark corners of the room brighten. The predawn quietude explodes with bustle. Suddenly the room cannot contain my spirit.

I want to burst out the doors.

Careen into the last of the night.

Do things.

Go places.

I look up just as Ed's face reappears from behind the smoke, a hissing from his lips, his eyes glowing with exhilaration.

What a great feeling!

I love Ed!

I love the whole fucking free world!

"Where did you get this stuff?" I pant.

"There's a place a few blocks from here," he breathes back.

"You gotta go anywhere?" I ask.

"As a matter of fact," he says, "I wanted to ask if I could crash here a few days."

He tries to explain about an argument with his people in Jersey, about them asking him to leave. But I wave him off in mid sentence, walk over to him, hug him chest to chest.

"Brother," I coo, "me and you are going to par-TEE!"

A few minutes later the bottom starts to fall out of the high.

Sadness and longing descend over me.

Utter desolation hovers moments away.

I am seized by a wave of panic.

I want that party feeling back.

"Listen, Ed," I say, "those guys still out? Can we get more—now?"

"Sure," he says.

I dig into my pocket and hand him the first fifty of the more than one hundred thousand dollars I will eventually smoke up before the party really ends.

Act III. Nine Months Later. *It is an early weekday morning. I lie sleeping on the platform bed in the back of my studio apartment. Except for a few essential furnishings, like the empty, half-size refrigerator by the stove, the room is uncommonly bare.*

No TV, no cable box, no radio. Not even a clock. They have all been either stolen or sold. Only unlaundered clothing, carelessly strewn here and there, and the debris of hurried, impromptu meals are in good evidence.

It is a first-floor apartment in the rear of a renovated, five-story walk-up on East Ninety-Sixth Street. One block shy of the projects that demarcate the northern tip of Yorkville from the southern edge of Spanish Harlem. They get close to nine hundred dollars a month for this single room.

And I'm a good three and a half months delinquent.

Biggie, my sometime dealer, is sprawled on the couch across the room from me. He is big, as the name implies, in a short, stout, chesty sort of way. Late last night he rang my buzzer and told me "work" was coming (meaning a bundle of crack was on its way) and if I let him wait inside for it, I'd get hit off with a free dime.

This has proved to be a ruse.

He needs a place to crash.

Pitchers (street-level dealers) don't clock the real paper.

After hours of anxious waiting, his subterfuge becomes obvious. But I'm too smoked out and defeated to challenge him on it. Ergo his prone, shirtless, Hershey-bar mass on my battered couch.

Out like a light.

When the doorbell rings, he is oblivious. But it brings me to a rude awakening. I drag myself over to the intercom.

"Yes?"

It's the marshal come to repossess the apartment.

I have been expecting him since the seventy-two-hour notice four days ago.

I say and do nothing.

My urge is to stave off the inevitable for as long as possible, and I take momentary refuge in the two doors standing between me and him. The front door is only plate glass, but my apartment door is the kind you find in the less tame regions of the city. Made of sheet steel and equipped with a police lock that bolts right into the frame.

I hear the front door squeak open and slam shut.

I hear the squeak of approaching feet in the hall.

In the peephole I can see the marshal looming up, his face distorted to hound-dog proportions.

He raps sharply on the door with some small, metallic object. This rouses Biggie. I can hear him stirring behind me.

"It's the marshal," I tell him. "He's come to take the apartment." Only

31

the way I say it, it could just as well be the mailman.

"Shit!" Biggie squeaks. "You better open that door. Them guys don't play. They carry guns, too."

Ready firepower.

The quintessence of authority in Biggie's trade.

But there is one thing I absolutely do not want to do at this moment. I do not want to open the door.

The marshal pounds again, this time promising we can do it "the hard way" if I want. "It's all up to you."

Biggie, who has already muscled back into his T-shirt, starts going fidgety, staring anxiously at the door as if we had a couple of keys of uncut Colombian stashed in the mattress.

It's a wonder to see this reaction from a guy who routinely plies his wares right across the street from the Housing Police precinct. I feel a detached amusement, a perverse flash of superiority even, over this jittery "gangsta"-in-residence.

But then I figure maybe he knows something I don't.

I defer to his greater street knowledge.

Undo the police lock.

Open the door.

The marshal steps in bristling, eyes already embarking on a tour of appraisal. He flashes a paper bearing the seal of the City of New York, proclaims he has been empowered by the court to take possession of the premises, informs me I have fifteen minutes to grab what I can, and cautions me to "do your talking walking."

Half an hour later I'm on the street, clutching a voucher for all that remains of my worldly possessions. Only instead of feeling put out, I feel strangely relieved. Elated even. I have just been released, I realize, from all earthly claims upon me.

There is nothing, anymore, that I am obliged to do.

No one, anymore, I am required to be.

Off to the freedom of the streets! *I tell myself.* Off to whatever happens next.

3

The Streets of New York City, 1985. As far as I was concerned, living on the streets was not an insurmountable inconvenience. There were some rough days, before I learned the ins and outs of soup kitchens and such. But once I hooked into picking up cans at a nickel a pop, I couldn't even be bothered with that cattle-call ordeal. And what a pleasure it was to sleep rent- and worry-free under the stars of Central Park.

Then one day the heels on my twenty-four-ninety-five-on- special Fayva shoes caved in. Soon after that the soles sprang open as well, and I couldn't imagine how I would get up the cash to replace them while going barefoot. So I asked around on the street where I might come by a pair of freebies, and was steered toward the Bowery.

"That's where they got all them missions," I was told.

Surprisingly no one on the subway seemed to notice my bare feet when I made the fifty-block trip from midtown to the Lower East Side. I stumbled around down there until I came upon a ragtag queue of Bowery bums in front of a white two-story stucco building. It turned out this was the well-known Bowery Mission. And their nine-to-five was helping down-on-their-luck types like me.

"You can get clothes in here?" I asked the weathered grapehead teetering on his feet at the end of the line, too-big clothes hanging off his bones. He must have been well into his third bottle of the day. I could barely decipher what he said. But I seemed to hear something of the affirmative in his din. So I joined him on line.

We were each issued a ticket at the door, assembled in the day room, then dispatched, ten at a time, to a modest dining room in the back. It was a makeshift meal, cadged together from many sources, but it was filling and satisfying.

After everyone was fed, they opened up the storeroom where they kept a supply of donated clothes. But I was out of luck. Size thirteen-and-a-half wide are not easy to come by. I spent the afternoon in their day room, slouched in a chair, drifting in and out of sleep. At one point I opened my eyes to see a pair of young slicksters straddling some old geezer who was off somewhere in dreamland. Curious, I watched them through the lashes of one half-opened eye.

Evidently whatever they were up to required much preliminary bickering. They stood there, one on either side of their quarry, scowling and hissing at each other, until whatever was their bother got itself resolved. Then the guy on the right reached out and, holding taut the fabric of their mark's trousers with one hand and wielding a single-edge razor like a surgeon with the other, neatly laid the pocket open.

I would have thought it a fruitless business; thievery in a place like this. But lo and behold, they came up with a fistful of random coins and crumpled bills. They scurried out the door after that like they had just knocked over a Brink's truck.

A man across the room, long face, drooping mustache, cap drawn over his eyes, looked my way, shaking his head solemnly from side to side.

"That's the trouble with us black folk," he said. "Always victimizing our own. Why don't they steal from the white man? White man got all the money!"

Growing up, whenever I mentioned a new schoolmate, my mother would ask, "What flavor? Chocolate or vanilla?" If I answered vanilla, she would raise her eyebrows. "I'll bet you *they* have money," she'd exclaim. I never did like what that implied about my own prospects. And I liked it a lot less sitting barefoot in the day room of the Bowery Mission. I might have called Longface on it, but looking around me, I couldn't see anything that might contradict his assumptions.

Instead I asked him where I could get some shoes.

"Just down the street," he told me. "City-run shelter on East Third Street. Anything you need."

The Bowery Intake Center on East Third was typical of the Depressingly Utilitarian school of urban municipal architecture. And through its ugly, turd-colored doors trudged a noticeably more desolate and desperate breed, it seemed, than I had seen at any of the privately run places. Those who couldn't—or wouldn't—enter its hallowed halls had set up a cardboard squatters' shantytown between the Dumpsters parked along the outside walls; a tableau that had *discarded* written all over it.

Inside, a limp-lidded security guard pointed the way into a large dim, spiritless box of a room, distressed, fifties-vintage, vinyl-aluminum chairs scattered ad hoc, listless human forms slumped in them. Lethargy pervaded the room like a fog. People stood twenty deep, numb, impatient, before a bank of lead-glass windows at the front of the room, the workers behind them indifferently plodding through the rigors of state-sanctioned, pro-forma Samaritanism.

I walked over to the only vacant window—the one with a handwritten sign designating it number one—tapped on the glass, and was greeted by a scowl that said, *Don't do that!* Then a form slid through a slot at the base of the window. I was told to fill it out—which I did promptly—and was just as promptly told to wait until I was called.

This turned out to be a matter of several long hours, during which I sat on the floor, slumped against the wall, being jostled rudely awake by the guard and told "No sleeping" whenever I drifted off. When I finally heard my name blasted over the speakers, I resolved to keep things as simple as possible.

"All I need is a pair of shoes," I told the lady behind Window 2. "They don't even have to be fresh out of the box."

A bemused twinkle came to her eyes. "It don' work this way," she said, a hint of the islands in her voice as she announced with some pride, "We have a system here. Intake. Meal ticket. Shelter voucher. You want us to help you, you do the whole ting."

By three o'clock I had been hooked up with the works and bussed up to Ward's Island—right across the East River from my former Ninety-sixth Street apartment ironically—accompanied by a hairy, spike-thin white guy who wasn't even on the same planet and a talky, blubberous, Jheri-curled brother of ambiguous sexuality. We were each subjected to a pat-down search, followed by a grave quickie lecture on the prohibitions of bringing contraband into the shelter, and were then told someone would be out to get us. The big queen chirped away as we waited on a bench just inside the complex, taking a certain pride in his extensive knowledge of the workings of the shelter system. He was obviously a regular.

"You are about to enter the *Waldorf* of city shelters," he informed me. "This here's as good as it gets."

"And who are you?" I asked him, "the Zagat of the down-and-out?"

He found that one doggone funny. Slapped me on my thigh and yucked it up. When a worker came out to fetch the white kid, it was "Would you follow me, please, Mr. Williams?" But when he came back later to fetch one of us, it was "Yo cuz, wanna come this way?"

Both Zagat and I thought that was a scream.

I was the last one in; ushered into a large, prison-style shower room, issued soap, a towel, delousing agent, and told to strip and shower. I was immensely grateful for the shower. I stepped from it feeling human again.

I was then given a handwritten ticket and sent upstairs, where I was issued underwear, a shirt, slacks, socks, and, at last, a pair of shoes. Secondhand, Oxford-brown, penny loafers to be exact—minus the pennies. I was also assigned a bed number and told to be in by nine o'clock or my bed would go to someone else.

"And remember," they added. "If you go out, you can't come back in for an hour. Same thing once you come in. Can't go out for an hour. Got it?"

I got it.

Up in the dorm I was offered a bargain on a bologna and cheese on white by an enterprising Puerto Rican fellow, running what seemed to be a lucrative trade selling cut-rate sandwiches out of his locker. I was hungry, but I declined. Thoughts of jockstraps and old Nikes commingling with the food kept insinuating themselves.

A little later a purveyor's truck rolled up to the back of the building and off-loaded an awesome shitload of food, huge bags of rice, sacks of potatoes, whole hams, turkeys, and roasts, industrial-size cans of fruit and vegetables, two-gallon jugs of milk. *That's the end of Slick's sandwich trade,* I thought to myself.

Only, in the four meals I had there, none of that stuff ever showed up on our plates. Breakfast was composed of a minibox of cereal, a half pint of milk, and a piece of fruit. Lunch and dinner were the same—a large serving spoon's worth of three-bean salad, three slices of fried salami, and two slices of bread.

"We won't see none of that," declared Zagat when I told him about the truck. (And let's face it, if he was an authority on anything, it would be food.) "Most of that stuff is going out the other door."

"No way," I said. "The Volunteers of America run this place for the city. A nonprofit."

"Nonprofit, huh?" Zagat said with a sigh. "Look. They make money on us. The city pays them for every swinging dick that comes through the door. Pays for all them goodies you saw coming in too. Probably selling the shit, for all I know."

I nodded, but I was having a hard time buying it.

"Don't believe me," Zagat said. "Tell you what. Go into the kitchen and tell them you want you a pork chop. Go ahead. Boy, they'll look at you like you're out your mind. 'A pork what? Nigger, you better *get* outta here and get your black ass a job!'"

The way he said it, I cracked up.

"It's all a hustle, brother," Zagat went on. "Without us all these people wouldn't have their jobs. They *need* folks like us. Me, I hustle 'em right back. I *get* mines. Already got three digits going under different names"—*Digits* being welfare benefits—"I were you, I'd get it now, brother. While you can. 'Cause I'll tell you. Pretty soon? This shit?"—

41

he said this, taking in the universe in one expansive sweep of his arm—
"Gonna be dead. These new people coming in? Uh-uh, honey. They're
fixin' to *kill* all this welfare shit."

Later that day I discovered my locker had been gone through.
I didn't have all that much of anything. All the same, I slept with my
stuff tucked underneath the mattress that night. I didn't stay another
night. I didn't like the karma of the place, for want of a better way to
put it—the guards, the pat-downs, the food lines, the whole, watch-
your-back, watch-your-mouth, watch-out-for-number-one, jailhouse
mentality. I figured I'd just as well take my chances on the street. But
my day and a half of sheltered life did confirm what had been hinted
at in the pocket incident at the Bowery Mission. That even at the
very bottom of existence it's still all about money.

The next day I donned my original clothes, which they had laun-
dered for me, and the secondhand, Oxford-brown penny loafers minus
their eponymous coins, and left behind my voucher, my meal ticket,
my clothing issue, and everything else they had given me.

4

Grand Central Terminal, Winter 1985, 12:30 a.m.

Already the police have begun to roust people from Grand Central Terminal for closing. I've just come from Central Park. When I went to dig up my trunk from where I keep it stashed in the bushes, it was gone. I found it laid open and ransacked a few yards away. Perhaps some other soul will be warm tonight, snuggled under my three thick army blankets.

I have struck up a conversation with a young brother from Jamaica, the two of us strolling as casually as we can, circling the terminal, keeping a step ahead of the encroaching cops. He's a happy-go-lucky type with a simple story. A painter by trade, his "woo-man" has kicked him out of the house. It will be a few days before he can collect his pay, so, like me, he is out on his ass.

He's no novice, however. He has been here before.

There have been other women, it appears, in other apartments, on whose whims the fortunes of this girl-toy-of-the-islands have risen or fallen. He just takes it as it comes.

Neither of us relishes the prospect of being turned out into the brisk December night, and he has a plan. I follow along as he steals, with authority, down two levels, across several track beds, until we are in a deserted corridor that leads to a little-used machine shop, gated and locked for the night. When I plop down on the floor, the cement sucks the heat right out of my ass. But a few pieces of cardboard and several minutes later I'm out like I was laying up at the Plaza.

The next thing I know, something is hitting the bottom of my foot. I hear a voice say "hey" something. When I open my eyes, I see only bright light and blackness beyond. Jamaica stirs a few feet away and the light swings over to him. I can now make out two men behind it, one pink-faced, short, dirty-gray on top, the other dumpy, baby-faced, blond bangs.

"Whaa...?" Is all that comes out of my mouth.

But they flash a shield and I know what's up.

The fat one comes on smug and condescending.

"'Sup guys?" he says, his grin triumphant. We do not know it yet, but he is already calculating the overtime it will be worth to arrest the two of us.

This yields a few moments' awkward silence.

He is not exactly a mental whiz.

The graytop is quiet and pouty.

He's a drinker.

I can tell this.

He could care less about the extra money. Right now he's

thinking about when he can be cut loose to pursue some uninter-
rupted tippling.

They go through our pockets methodically, extract an item, hold
it up to the flashlight, toss it on the floor. There is nothing of any real
consequence in my pockets. But it is my property nonetheless. It irks
me that they treat it with such unnecessary disdain. No sooner have
I worked up a healthy resentment over this than they are clicking on
the cuffs.

"You're under arrest for criminal trespass" is all they say. No "right
to remain silent" business. Nothing about an attorney. The whole matter is too trivial for all that.

We are led up to their third-floor headquarters, which has the
distinction of having once been the private apartment of one of the
Vanderbilts.

"See?" the fat one says to his partner while hauling us in. "You
make money when you're with me." Partner, tagging sullenly along,
only nods, eyes glued to the floor.

We are put in a holding cell with another pair of ragged souls
and treated to the police version of the cabbie's "scenic route." They
stretch out the booking process beyond tolerance. Fatso waddles up
to our cell, asks a question, disappears for twenty minutes, then returns
for another one.

While this act is going on, their captain pops in briefly. He struts
through the place playing Good Cop to the hilt. One of us has money

and asks him if he can use the vending machine sitting in the corner of the room.

This seems to perplex him.

Perhaps he is a sergeant, not a captain.

After mulling it over for a good while he disappears, returning ten minutes later with a box of glazed doughnuts and—don't ask me by what process of thought he arrives at this incidental bit of democracy—he passes them out to all of us.

We eat them cuffed.

Crumbs and flakes of sugar-glaze raining over everything.

They get about five hours out of all this, then drive us down to Central Booking in Chinatown. It's a busy night. The explosion of crack cocaine has been something of a boon for the criminal justice system. The admitting officer groans when he sees the Metro North cops, us in tow, and shakes his head in disgust.

"Whaddya got here, more homeless? For Chrissake!"

"They're good collars," the fat one whines like a wannabe.

But nobody's really listening.

In the main holding cell they are packed in shoulder-to-shoulder. Despite the raggedness of our little group, we are treated with surprising respect by the other prisoners, offered cigarettes, and given their unwanted sandwiches at feeding time.

All in the same boat now, I guess.

No matter what your game is on the street.

It will take three days to get out of there. But, being my first time, I can't know this. The uncertainty as to what will happen makes for an agonizing eternity of waiting. Every hour or so the CO stalks in, thunderously slams the cell gate a few times to rouse the sleeping, and calls out a dozen names for transport to the courthouse.

I try to catch up on my sleep in forty-five-minute segments.

When Jamaica and I finally reach the court building, my appointed attorney assures us we will be going home.

"I don't even see why they arrested you in the first place," he says. "They could have served you with a summons."

"Overtime," I tell him.

He nods knowingly.

A few minutes later we appear before the judge and are cut loose with little ceremony. Our transgression is too inconsequential to offer any real sport to the vast assemblage of earnest law servers. We dash to midtown with our court-issued tokens, Jamaica ducks into his place of employ, emerges with hard cash, and we hit the deli two doors down.

We chow down in a corporate, public-space-type "park," whose nod to nature is a few scattered potted plants about the concrete and a man-made waterfall, which dampens the surrounding traffic din. Although we are broke and homeless, the greasy chicken and cold potato salad tastes sweet with freedom.

It is several months later, a red-letter day for me at Grand Central; the height of the rush hour, a major interruption of service on all Metro North trains, and nothing is going in or out. Commuters are piling up in the main concourse, spilling over into the north and south corridors. Every bar cart, delicatessen, and food shop is mobbed. Soda and beer are going at the rate of sixty a minute.

That's $180 in empties per hour.

I know this because I have stood watching the checkouts at Zaro's, the Terminal Deli, and the bar carts long enough that I can extrapolate an aggregate rate for the entire terminal.

It is a trick I developed while doing advertising and marketing at a small consumer products start-up called United Products. We had been riding a wave of success with a product called Free Support. I had worked on most of its development, and when it came to estimating what its sales prospects might be, I had to project from small samples and what little general data were available. Who would have imagined this would have any application on the street?

Empties are scattered everywhere.

It is even better than New Year's Eve, when I scored $100 worth of cans in a couple of hours. I have already filled one industrial-size plastic baggie (good for twenty dollars), and half of another. Behind the departure gates, stalled travelers linger along the platforms, impatient for any sign of a train. I squeeze my way around, between, and through them. Some acknowledge my industry by surrendering their empties. A few act as spotters, alerting me to cans they have sighted.

But mostly I am anonymous; invisible. They see only a phenomenon to which they have already adjusted. I make no deeper impression on their consciousness than the taxicabs, endlessly cruising outside, do on pedestrians.

But as I make my way back toward the gate, I am noticed.

A man in a dark business suit.

I know him.

For a second I burn with embarrassment; the old me, the one who measured men by the cut of their suits, is ashamed to be caught so lowly. Yet, just as quickly, I am again the new me, the one shorn of his props, and I am looking at the old me's former boss.

"Wajdi," I say, with now-casual surprise.

"How are you, Lee?" he says. He has a quick and disarming smile. I shrug. What can I say?

"So you are collecting cans?"

Before I can catch myself, I launch into a slightly manic resume of the ins and outs of my present vocation, and the money it yields. Wajdi's eyebrows fly skyward, impressed, not by the amount itself—hardly a decimal point in the scheme of his riches—but that it can be gleaned from such a niggardly source.

"You know that old sales letter you left on the computer?" he asks. "I use it as a model for all my sales letters." This brings back the old me, the logos, ads, packaging, and displays I designed; the sales letters, marketing plans, consumer surveys.

"You know, there is nothing in the company that doesn't have your hand in it," Wajdi says. "You were really brilliant."

I shrug again. But I am flattered.

"But tell me," he says, his eyes dipping down to the bag over my shoulders, "don't you miss it?"

I tell him I am no less happy now than I was then.

"And to tell the truth," I add, "I wasn't all that happy then."

I tell him that I don't find living on the street a major inconvenience.

I tell him I am a survivor.

"But doesn't your brain atrophy?" he asks.

I tell him quite the contrary.

I tell him that there are new challenges every day.

I tell him that away from the lull of routine, one must be on one's toes.

He accepts this with equanimity.

He may have a few million under his belt.

But he is no snob.

We talk on for a few minutes and then he departs, wishing me well. I am grateful that he does not offer me a handout, even though it's for certain that had he, I would have taken it.

I proceed down the platform with renewed energy.

There is money to be made.

5

Grand Central Terminal, Winter 1989. I suppose Mr. Waldorf—I call him that because he turned out to be the human resources manager for the famous hotel (which is a fancy way of saying he hired the help)—thought Craig and I were heroes that night on the ramp at Grand Central.

I thought Waldorf was...perhaps "foolish" is too unkind. "Naive," let's say—parading around midtown in the wee hours, telltale white powder lining his nostrils. To the two mopes who decided to vic him (as in *victimize*) the guy was just asking for it.

But heroes?

Craig and me?

We just had lousy choices.

It was only a matter of circumstance that we were where we were that night. It had been a bitter winter. And the only thing between us and the cold was the oak and glass doors that opened onto Grand Central Station and the subway.

The terminal closed promptly every night. From one-thirty to five-thirty in the morning. But the subway runs twenty-four/seven. So the intervening ramp, situated between the terminal's great outer doors and the steel gates that kept us from its inner reaches, served—for those of us with no other place to go—as a handy place to catch a few hours' fitful sleep .

Craig and I had become fast friends one afternoon while perched on the pew-like benches inside the terminal's main waiting room. He had been laid off from Gimbel's department store when they shut down in order to cash in on the real estate they were occupying. And, one thing leading to another, he wound up on the street.

As far as I could tell, he had not developed the predator's instincts by which many of Grand Central's squatters survived. And though he was about my size, over six feet tall, he was unassuming and soft-spoken. The type to keep to his own concerns. Which is why it took me by surprise, that night on the ramp, when he made his move.

We hung out together because I had introduced him to what I called the franchise. You see, ninety thousand people hurl through Grand Central each day and they drink a lot of soda and beer. Each empty can or bottle they leave in their wake is worth a nickel redemption. All one has to do is harvest them and take them to the supermarket.

This is no secret.

However, I discovered one day, quite by accident—and here's the "franchise" part—that at the far end of one platform, beyond where any passenger need or dare venture, sat a number of open-topped "gondola" railroad cars, all heaped with industrial-size garbage bags pregnant with rubbish, the bulk of which was discarded newspapers and cans. A few hours sorting through this relatively mild refuse yielded me a good thirty to forty dollars.

The cars also always contained several boxes of completely wrapped and sealed sandwiches, snacks, and dinners from Amtrak cafe and dining cars, which, due to the miracle of expiration dating, became legally unsalable at the stroke of that day's midnight.

Amtrak's loss was my gain, as I figured it, and Craig and I bought ourselves much easy popularity hauling this stuff out to the main waiting room for the others. Many was the day we fed every hungry homeless soul in Grand Central with what was, to Amtrak railroad, so much garbage.

It hadn't been too long before that we could have camped out on the benches of Grand Central's main waiting room at night. Mayor Koch himself had promoted this idea, reasoning that the terminal was, after all, closed and idle for four hours every night; what more appropriate use of a public space than to shelter those who had become, in essence, public people?

It proved to be a short-lived arrangement.

For no provisions had been made for the fact that we would still be there when the terminal opened in the morning, and that, it being winter at the time, a good number of us would elect to stay for the remainder of the day.

Among other things, this caused a mob scene in the bathrooms each morning as dozens of us literally bathed and did our laundry in the sinks—a spectacle that fairly rattled early-bird commuters. Feeding ourselves would be next on the agenda, through whatever mechanism of survival we had each developed.

Panhandlers would descend on the commuters.

Petty thieves would hover near deli counters, seeking an opportune moment.

Others would ravage Dumpsters and trash cans for refundable containers or a scrap of uneaten food.

And in this frenzy, which in the dawning hours was at its most intense, frustration and bad will percolated.

It wasn't long before terminal shopkeepers made it clear to Metro North management that—Grand Central's public mission notwithstanding—they did not pay their exorbitant rents to be greeted by a ragged, often impudent horde of indigents each morning.

Shortly thereafter the purge began.

Signs were posted in the bathrooms prohibiting bathing, laundering, shaving, loitering, and any other activity short of pissing and shitting.

Zaro's bakery encased their ostentatious displays of goodies beneath see-through Plexiglas and doused all their edible discards with used coffee grinds to render them inedible.

Metro North police outlawed all activities peculiar to homeless people. "Loitering," panhandling, garbage browsing, and sleeping became grounds for expulsion or, in some cases, deliberately rough-handed arrest.

Management methodically eliminated every conceivable horizontal surface, closed the waiting room for "repairs," and banned sitting on the floors.

It also became a matter of policy that everyone but railroad employees vacate the terminal precisely at closing. And to urge everyone's compliance, terminal police made rounds every night, a half hour in advance, armed with snarling, German shepherd K-9s.

In the face of all this, whatever bad will had existed before now turned more adversarial and meaner in spirit.

I never elected to sleep in the waiting room myself.

The place was the scene of a continuous, boisterous, often drunken, bacchanal. And while that could be a lot of fun during the day, it was not conducive to more restful pursuits. I preferred sleeping on the lower-level platform under a stairwell. There was a cubbyhole beneath the platform where I could store things as well.

Later Craig slept down there, too, and we were able to watch each other's back. Over time we became more than friends. We became partners in survival—which came in handy those later nights on the ramp. For the ramp crowd was composed, for the most part, of the former waiting-room horde, now hardened by the new order of things and none the nicer for the trip. And added to their number were a handful of serpentine souls, who spent each night slouched just inside the doors, basking in the sanctuary from police scrutiny that the ramp offered, peering like vultures through the wired glass, seeking any opportunity to "get paid."

You see, the ramp encompassed an area where the jurisdictions of the Metro North, Transit, and city police departments converged. And as none of them were particularly keen on taking charge of us nightly squatters, it became a kind of demilitarized zone. Only when day broke and the station opened would the transit police emerge and roust us from our perch.

Otherwise we sleeping dogs were left to lie.

But those of us not inclined to kidding ourselves knew it was just a matter of time before this, too, would be finished.

Waldorf was just a working grunt from the tip of New Jersey trudging homeward after a night of eighties excess when he happened upon this milieu. I suppose if the mayor of New York could have been so grandly naive, it is easy to understand Waldorf's hapless response.

The wind had pushed Craig and me indoors early that night. Our sleeping niche under the stairs had long ago been busted. So we had stashed the night's cache of cans and had idled in the warmth of the waiting room until the "Rin-Tin-Tin" squad brought on the hounds.

We then repaired to the ramp.

I was fast-bound for a good snooze when the terminal doors flew open, letting in an angry blast of wind that caused me to scrunch up tighter in an attempt to squeeze all of me under my overcoat, which was doubling as a blanket.

In trudged Waldorf, heading for the subway—a short, Ryan O'Neal-looking pup in a shiny, gray, entry-level power suit. One gander down the ramp and he stopped dead in his tracks, seemed to crumble, slightly, at the sight before him: twenty to thirty human beings—men, women, young bucks in their prime, wheezy matrons, pug-nosed (and pugnacious) old-timers, boozed-out winos, crashed-out crackheads, bewildered children—all huddled on the cold concrete floor of Grand Central's lower-level access ramp.

Frozen there, he moaned, "Oh. My. God!" in three succinct, trembling syllables. This was amplified to operatic proportions because he was coked-up, for one thing (I could make out the telltale halos of white), and also because the terminal's marble walls play Ping-Pong with sound.

"Oh my God," he repeated.

This time actually choking back a sob.

I remember thinking, *This guy's obviously no New Yorker.* After four years' exposure to "the homeless," sights like this had ceased to startle the rank and file of Gotham. Like Ellison's *Invisible Man,* we had receded into that part of the landscape that refused to support the American Dream.

And which few are wont to see.

Nonpeople in a no-man's void.

Of course indifference grows both ways. We, the wretched, had become just as adept at relegating the passing public to the periphery of *our* consciousness.

So, though the appalled Mr. Waldorf's bald exclamations roused me and several of my contemporaries, resounding as they did off the walls, it was by virtue of their volume rather than their sentiment.

It must have then occurred to Waldorf, teetering there at the head of the ramp, how perfectly situated he was to facilitate our salvation. And, seized by a sudden wave of altruism, he pulled his business cards from his pocket, started down the ramp, dropping them here and there like manna from heaven, proclaiming with earnest fervor that he had jobs for everyone who wanted them.

The result of all this was to rouse a few vague mumbles of protest from those who took exception to being so rudely tugged from their slumber.

But not all of us were intent on sleep.

At least two of us were not about to disdain an opportunity.

Just inside the doorway four anxious, predatory eyes floated over to Waldorf and parachuted down his body.

They took in the coke-caked nose.

Appraised the faux Armani suit and, taking the knockoff for the real thing, wondered about the depth of its pockets.

With a practiced precision, and without need for discussion between them, they both pressed something of a smile into service and, least forbidding one in the lead, casually sidled over to Waldorf.

"'Scuse me," they chirped, all syrup and cream, "but you would-n't happen to have any change you could spare, would you?"

Waldorf wasn't watching them watch him as his hand went crackling into his pocket and extracted a bill that obviously had not been lonely in there.

But Craig was watching.

He pounded my shoulder.

"Hey man," he whispered, "they're going to vic that guy."

I realized, to my surprise, that Craig was going to intervene. I also knew that if he did, there was no way I would sit it out. My instincts were against it. It had been my experience that jumping into someone else's business was a surefire way to earn the enmity of every-one involved. But before I could register these reservations, the two guys were on Waldorf. One had him by the throat from behind, and the other went for his pockets. Craig was already on his feet, charg-ing up the ramp.

I scrambled to catch up.

"Hey, guys," Craig said as we came up on them, his voice sur-prisingly calm. "This is not cool."

The two perps just glared hatred at us through the slits of their eyes, and clung fast to their startled quarry. An adrenaline rush was trembling through my body. I figured I could shoulder-tackle the guy in front if I had to, flip him over my back, and take him out before he knew what was happening.

Craig would have to take the other guy.

All I hoped was that I didn't get hit in the face.

I go ballistic when I get hit in the face.

"Not here," Craig went on as I stood by, trying my best to add silent menace to his words. "Do this shit outside. You'll ruin it for all of us. We got to sleep here."

At this point we had something of an audience.

About ten pairs of barely opened lids were now looking on. And they had all been alerted, by Craig's carefully chosen words, of the stake they had in the outcome of this thing.

I could see in the choke-holder's face that he was calculating the odds against him and his boy. And after a few seconds of taut silence, he released the half nelson he had on Waldorf without protest. Then, sneering back at Craig and me, he and his partner back-pedaled to the subway and disappeared down the stairs.

Craig and I walked Waldorf outside.

I managed a few mumbled cautions to him against traipsing the streets skeed-up at this hour (as if Craig and I hadn't done precisely the same thing numerous times ourselves).

Craig chimed in on this too.

But, in truth, both of us—keenly aware of the fact that Waldorf liked to indulge—were hoping that, seeing as the excitement was over and we were wide awake and all, perhaps a grateful Mr. Waldorf might see his way clear to rewarding us with a toot or two of the white stuff.

We stood on either side of him, finessing this aspiration to the point of determining that he had none on him.

He had been out with his girl.

It was her stuff.

And now she and it were gone.

Instead Waldorf struck on another idea.

"You guys want jobs?" the human resources manager in him said. "You need a place to stay tonight? C'mon, you guys are coming with me."

A short ride on the PATH train, and we found ourselves in a small, one-bedroom walk-up, somewhere just over the Jersey line. What had run through my mind on the way over was that here was Waldorf, ushering into his home a pair of completely desolate strangers he had just met on a ramp at Grand Central, right after a near mugging at the hands of another pair of ramp-rovers.

Some people never learn.

Not that he had all that much to burglarize, if we had been so inclined. His humble furnishings and the pile of unopened bills I later noticed on his wood-grain veneer dresser told me that the distance between his predicament and ours was not so great as one might think.

Having said that, however, I hasten to add that as overnight accommodations go, his place beat any other I had had that winter hands down. And in all fairness, Waldorf had reason to think that Craig and I were trustworthy, since we had just intervened on his behalf.

But it was also true that our actions were self-serving as much as anything else. The interests we considered, however they may have co-joined with Waldorf's, were our own, and what risks we took were calculated.

It had been a pitiless winter.

We knew that as soon as they were armed with a few complaints, the authorities would put an end to our tenuous tenancy just inside the doors of New York's biggest public mansion. Our impulse, therefore, had been to save ourselves.

So, no, though Waldorf might be inclined to argue to the contrary, Craig and I were not guilty of heroism. Heroism, as I see it, requires a deliberate decision to assume avoidable risks specifically—not incidentally—for the sake of another.

By that measure we were at best guilty of heroics, which isn't the same thing.

Nonetheless I slept on Waldorf's floor that night and yielded the couch to Craig in deference to the fact that it was his initiative that had gotten us there. Then, too, it was Craig who got hired as an elevator operator when we applied at the Waldorf Hotel the next day. They tried to placate me with the "overqualified" bit as they showed me the door.

After that, Craig and I gradually went our separate ways. I continued to work "the franchise" for nickels and dimes, while he spent his days gainfully brownnosing the chic and beautiful of the Waldorf as he ferried them skyward.

6

West Forty-sixth Street, Winter 1989. The *Street News* distribution office is located in a midtown storefront on Manhattan's West Side, formerly the site of a Blimpie's sandwich shop, long ago gone belly-up. The cracked plastic sign still hangs above the door. Inside, the place has been gutted, giving it a makeshift quality quite appropriate to the cause.

The first time I laid eyes on this place, a pair of old street geezers were perched on upturned milk crates just outside the door, oblivious to the winter chill, garbed in black caps, T-shirts, and money aprons that said *Street News*. Each had a wad of bills pinched between his fingers and they were comparing the thicknesses of their respective accumulated earnings. I was struck by the brilliance of their gap-toothed grins. Trailing out the door and snaking halfway down the block was a line of eager people waiting to get in, all summoned there by nothing more than word of mouth. The whole scene had an exhilarating, up-from-the-streets kind of momentum, reminiscent of the phenomenon now offhandedly dismissed as the sixties.

Only, the eighties were in good evidence as well.

The place reeked of commerce.

Money poured in in its most visible form.

In thick, crinkled wads of green.

Even the smell of coffee and bacon that greeted you as you opened the door was a matter of enterprise. One of the vendors had set up a hot plate and enjoyed a thriving trade selling meals to the mushrooming sales force.

We all had money to burn.

Street News was sweet news.

We bought the papers for a quarter each, sold them for seventy-five cents. Three bucks for every dollar invested. The papers flew out of our hands, for all over the city the streets were filled with home-lessness and compassion. Even a mindless shnook can take home sixty dollars a day. For those of us with demons to feed, the easy money rendered thoughts of larceny obsolete, and for those who suffered only from cruel circumstance, it was a chance to once again dare to flirt with dreams.

I'd thought I had it pretty good with "the franchise." But Grand Central management and the supermarkets where I cashed in my cans no longer wanted anything to do with folks like me. And by wielding their almighty "rules of conduct," they virtually conspired to make it all but impossible for us to earn a decent buck.

I still managed to scare up maybe twenty-five bucks a day. But the risk of arrest was greater than it had been—not to mention the long hours spent toting my cans from store to store, due to the supermarket's new prohibition against redeeming more than a dollar's worth at a time.

I'd run into Craig just before Christmas.

"Still doing the cans, eh?" he said.

He had been fired from the Waldorf, before he could get himself a place to live. He had come in late once too often. Working nine-to-five and living on the street don't mix.

"But I've got a new hustle now," he told me, and pulled out a copy of *Street News*. "You'll make mad money," he sang. "Better than doing cans."

Odd thing was, some part of me took this as a slight. (Funny, the things a man will take pride in doing.) But it had been cat-and-mouse all day with the Metro North cops. I had been warned that if I were caught on the platforms one more time, they'd lock me up. So I decided to give *Street News* a shot.

My first customer was a handsomely groomed dowager with an apple-cheek smile. She handed me a ten-dollar bill, goodwill wafting off her like a perfume, and told me I'd better keep the change.

I envied the joy she took in giving.

And I had to admit, pride or no, *Street News* sure beat the hell out of picking cans.

But it's not just the easy money.

For most of us vendors this old Blimpie's was like our clubhouse. We lingered here when we came for papers, milled around, worked the winter chill from our bones, traded stories of the street. Within the bare and charred walls, we could emerge from the dark of our aloneness. Who are the true homeless anyway but people trying desperately to live alone?

A car rolled up to the curb.

Out leaped Hutchinson Persons, founder of *Street News*.

He strode triumphantly through the doors, long hair trailing in the wind. A blond messiah for the lowly.

We flocked to him.

—Hutch! Hutch!

—Did you see my name in the *Post*?

—I have something you should put in the paper!

—When's the next issue coming out?

Hutch didn't quite know how it had come to this. He only wanted to put on the world's biggest show. A concert for the hungry. Put his name in lights. Get himself to where he wanted to go. Sure, feed a few people in the bargain. Only he never meant to adopt this needy horde. Now notoriety had rained down on him. The world now thought he was the man with The Plan.

And he would surely try.

But he didn't see, exactly, or perhaps couldn't bring himself to trust, what was right in front of his eyes.

"You guys are doing a terrific job!" he said.

And this was butter on our bread.

There were fresh papers to unload.

"Twenty freebies go to anyone who will help."

There was a fair stampede of activity. In minutes the papers got hustled inside. We lined up for the giveaway. Hutch stood behind the makeshift wood-plank counter and "knighted" us each in turn with our bounty. Then he huddled with the staff, checking that all was in order. We stayed put, murmuring among ourselves. We weren't in any hurry. We knew the money would be out there. Right then we were content to savor the feeling, so recent and so rare, of having it all in front of us.

"What are you guys hanging around for?" Hutch asked, but not in an unkindly way. "Why aren't you out there selling papers?"

A few men looked to the floor, dutifully embarrassed but not exactly sure why. We made much business of going, gathering our papers together, pulling on our caps, eyes wandering to the doorway with mild distress. I buttoned up, slow and reluctant. I couldn't put my finger on precisely what was so special about this patched-together place.

"Keep up the good work," offered Hutch as his fingers climbed the buttons on his coat.

Then he made for the car.

Spun away from the curb.

None of us knew it yet, but soon Hutch would actually try to do the thing he never set out to do. He had heard that we needed to be saved from ourselves, and he was going to give it the good college try.

Soon everything would change.

The hot plate would have to go.

There would be no hanging around allowed.

No pestering him with our vague ideas.

Soon it would no longer be our place.

It would be like the crack spots.

Just cop and go.

7

In New York City there are three centers for people living on the street: Central Park, Grand Central Terminal, and Central Booking.

This last is the city's own private purgatory. A timeless void between apprehension and judgment. When you finally emerge—ragged, unwashed, and hungry—into the crisp, efficient courtroom, you can easily see why everyone there treats you like a less evolved life-form.

The cops hardly need a reason to put street people in this place these days. But I gave them one anyway. I tried to swing a free ride on the subway by slipping through the turnstiles without paying.

It was "sweep" day.

I was swept.

Sitting in the holding pen with a hundred or so other souls snatched from the streets, I tried, for the sake of serenity, to strike a balance between the expectations of our keepers outside the cage and those of us on the inside. An impossible task, but we can always hope. So far, in my previous transits through "the system," I had been spared confrontation. There were others around me who had not been quite so fortunate. Periodic bitching, moaning, and scrapping erupted, most of it minor, and to my way of thinking, petty and unnecessary. Not that my way of thinking held any weight among my fellow captives. Which is why I kept it to myself and otherwise tried to remain just another body. You were either a feeder or you were food in this place. I figured I'd keep them guessing.

Not like the Jersey kid sitting on the bench with that gold chain around his neck. I've seen plenty of gold flashed in Central Booking. Thick, gaudy ropes with saucer-sized medallions dangling from them; two- and three-finger rings monogrammed in block letters. But that's Bold Gold. Worn gangsta-style. Up-front and In-Your-Face.

Jersey's single meek "me too" strand only mocked him.

It was obvious to me he had never been arrested before. He jerked up, anxious and apprehensive, at any sudden noise, a captive with no idea what his captors had in store for him. It was just as obvious that he had been in a fight because of the white bandage tied, bandanna-style, around his forehead, through which had seeped a quarter-sized blotch of blood, long since dried. He had been in the middle of a bar-room brawl, I later found out, but his head wound was courtesy of the cops who had broken it up.

The wound was his good fortune, however. It implied that he was not a total stranger to mixing it up. And that bought him a mea-sure of slack from the grizzled veterans in whose midst he stood out like a sore thumb. The bad news was, an even more bloodied warrior would make it to Central Booking that night.

Early that evening the cell gates clanged open and the CO ushered in a thin, bare-chested Spanish kid wearing hospital-green pajama bottoms splattered with crimson. His arms were swathed, wrist to elbow, in bandages and he was grinning ear to ear.

"They had to keep my shirt for evidence," he announced to no one in particular, holding his damaged arms aloft like trophies. Then, without prompting, he launched, with relish, into his war story. He and his crew were doing a burglary...the cops had surprised them in the middle of it...he "took a bullet" in one arm trying to escape (a matter of particular pride) and had done-in the other arm scrambling over razor wire. They had to patch him up at Bellevue before they could book him. All in all, a Hollywood-worthy night out for a restless teen.

"They tell me I'm a career criminal," he gushed, "in-curr-ridge-i-ble."

Everyone was duly impressed. I was both captivated and unsettled by his moxy, though I never let on. From the corner of the cell, a few feet from where I sat hunched on the floor, someone called his name. His partners in the ill-fated enterprise had apparently been collared with less to-do. And having no need for a pit stop at Bellevue themselves, they had beaten The Kid downtown. It was an auspicious reunion. Hugs all around. A tiny tube of Vaseline lip balm appeared between them, and within seconds the three had slipped their slender hands out of their cuffs. I held my hands up in a "me too?" gesture. But his buddies, who up until then had been indistinguishable from the pack, had now taken on a smug swagger, basking, by association, in The Kid's glory.

They waved me off like a pesky fly.

I was puffing on a cigarette, contemplating how much of it to leave for the guy who had begged the "short" from me, when I saw The Kid move for the Jersey boy.

"I like that rope, homeboy," he said, leaning his face into Jersey's. "Let me get that chain!" Something in his hand was pressing against Jersey's jugular.

Incorrigible.

This was just the thing to break the monotony of sitting on your butt awaiting the pleasure of the court. The holding cell sprang to life. A circle of inmates formed two deep around Jersey and The Kid. If we were going to be treated to a throw-down, they were determined to keep the COs at bay for as long as possible.

But Jersey had had enough fisticuffs for one night, apparently. He didn't give up the chain. But he did yell for help. I heard keys rattle in the gate. A second later, correction officers were elbowing their way through the human blockade. But The Kid, who could have easily ditched the shiv, remained oblivious to them. He just stood there menacing Jersey while the guards broke through and grabbed him. They recuffed him (tighter this time) and as they hauled him off to book him on an additional charge, I caught a glimpse of his face.

His smirk was wider than ever.

Most of us in that cell knew we could expect to walk. We knew if we just bided our time and let the criminal justice grind take its course, we could get back to whatever it was we were doing with a minimum of hassle. The Kid, though, knew he wasn't going anywhere. He was a "career criminal." He also knew that with his good looks, youth, and diminutive size, it was better to go inside with a "don't-give-a-fuck" bad-ass rep preceding him. In that respect he was, for all his bravado, only being practical, and buying in on the cheap for all that.

Jersey, on the other hand, was a novice. He wasn't quite sure where he'd be going. Just the type of guy this purgatory was designed for. It's the guilt, fear, and stones in your own heart that take you down. Seeing the judge is just a formality. By the time Jersey hit "the cage"— that little room in the court building where he'd be thrown together with a court-appointed lawyer and where his fate would really be determined—he'd be all theirs.

When it came my turn to appear before the judge, I took the advice of my counsel and fessed up to trying to steal a subway ride. The prosecutor declined, knowing I had already been through their purgatory, to recommend further incarceration, and I was free to go. But not before they gave me a free subway token to get home.

Being a minor-league "career criminal" myself, I bought five quarter snacks with the token and, figuring the odds were with me, hopped the turnstile for the trip uptown. As the No. 1 train rattled its way north, I wondered, for a moment, how Jersey had made out. I'd like to think I would have comported myself better than he did if it were my throat The Kid had a jagged edge against. Truth is, though, until I'm in the same predicament, I won't really know.

I guess it depends on what's at stake.

In all probability Jersey saw the judge, got spun out, and went back to Bayonne or wherever. And as long as he didn't look for any more trouble, he would never see the likes of Central Booking again.

But if he was headed for Rikers or the Tombs, either this time or in the near future, he was going to have a problem. The one rep you don't want to take with you to prison is that of a snitch. And calling for the guard as he did may have saved Jersey his jewelry, but it may yet cost him his jewels. The ones even the Bold Gold only symbolize.

That's not to say he'd had any easy choices.

When it comes to justice, the kind that gets you locked up is different from the kind you find inside. Personally I would like to see all judges and district attorneys made to do time. Not for the crimes they commit from the bench. For they commit those out of ignorance. Which is precisely why time in prison should be part of their qualifications. So that they might come to know what they don't know they don't know.

Let them sit faceless and despised in the holding cells, let them be run through the wringer of their process until the wind has been wrung out of their self-righteousness. And let them stumble on the wisdom every two-bit con knows instinctively, that real justice is always poetic.

Community Service, I. 60 Centre Street, 1994. It all

seemed so simple at the arraignment. My three minutes with a lawyer before going in to see the judge had been reassuring.

"We've got a sweetheart of a judge out there," he beamed.

He seemed to be a new breed of court-appointed lawyer, black, younger than usual, and lacking in smugness. In theory every accused is entitled to a trial. But for anything less than a serious felony, a trial's the last thing anyone wants. The name of the game is for the court to clear its docket. So it's good to have some idea of what you want in return for the expedience of plea.

What I wanted was to walk.

Trouble was I had been caught red-handed, right after copping ten dollars' worth of rock cocaine on the street. Walking away, marveling at the size of the rock in my hand, I heard the shuffle of running feet behind me and turned around just in time for two undercovers to tackle me to the ground.

"Here's our position," my lawyer said. "According to the police report, you had less than a quarter gram of controlled substance on you, which is nothing. If they want to make a case, they have to come up with a lab report and affidavits from both arresting officers in three

days. But the system is so backlogged, they don't sweat the little stuff."
He grinned like a co-conspirator. "All you have to do is wait it out
till Tuesday and they'll cut you loose."

"Tuesday?" I said. "Wait here till Tuesday?"

"Yeah, right upstairs in the Tombs."

But I couldn't afford to be locked up until Tuesday. I had to
put the next issue of *Street News* to bed. My editor was out of town
on vacation, leaving me in charge. I made no secret to her of my
being a cokehead, however short I might have been on the details.
And I had always consoled myself with the fact that at least it was-
n't at the expense of others. If I got locked up, that would no longer
be true.

I explained the predicament to the lawyer.

"If I'm not there, the next issue will not get to press," I lamented.
"And dozens of vendors will be left stuck."

Fortunately he was familiar with *Street News*. In fact he seemed
somewhat impressed.

"Ah, *Street News*," he exclaimed, eyebrows to the ceiling.

He mulled this over briefly and tried to walk me through the
give-and-take of the bail process. But that wasn't an option. I had all
of sixty dollars on me and nowhere to raise bail on a Friday night.

"Well, what you do have going for you," he finally said, "is that
you have an address, you're employed, an editor, a respected member
of the community. Chances are we can plea you out with time served.

And if they don't go for that, we can try to get you released on your own recognizance until your trial."

This perked me up a bit.

"If *that* doesn't work," he went on, taking in a good lungful of courthouse air, "we have one more option."

That's when he brought up community service. I'd get to do my bid during the day and go home at night.

"It'll be our last resort," he said.

But when we went before the "sweetheart" judge, she took one gander at the representative for Cases, a community service program—who had appeared somewhat prematurely, in my opinion, for a "last resort"—and she started talking tough.

Thirty-days-at-Riker's-Island tough, to be exact.

"Your Honor," my lawyer huffed, "I'm shocked you're even recommending time in this case. My client is the editor of *Street News.*" He announced this with such unbridled pride you would have thought I was the CEO of Time Warner. On he rambled for a moment or two about my being a respectable this and an upstanding that, a pitch so dim that it had the judge gazing wistfully out of the dirty courtroom windows.

This was followed by a spiritless back-and-forth about the advisability of bail, which died quickly once the prosecutor chimed in that I had ignored two previous desk-appearance citations for selling *Street News* on the subway.

I turned to my lawyer, who, having apparently exhausted his litigious repertoire proclaiming my sterling character, now seemed to be at a loss. We all stood there in silence for a moment. The judge, I suspect, took pity on my counsel, and was giving him a chance to offer something more substantial. But he just stood there blinking back at her like an admonished child. *That explains his lack of smugness,* I thought to myself. *He's probably never been in a courtroom before.*

Finally the judge threw him a lifeline.

"Ah, I see we have Cases in the courtroom," she said, peering over my lawyer's shoulder at the Cases representative hovering in the rear of the courtroom in a fresh gray suit.

Grateful beyond words for having been thrown this bone, my lawyer summoned him forth with a flurry of "come hither" hand motions, and eagerly yielded the floor to him.

After that everything proceeded briskly.

—Cases rep spoke to the judge.

—Judge spoke to the prosecutor.

—Prosecutor spoke to the judge.

—Judge spoke to my lawyer.

—My lawyer spoke to Cases rep.

It all seemed like a lively enough party. I only wished I had been invited. I could have been in Cleveland for all it mattered.

"In consideration of a plea of guilty," the judge said to me at last. "on the charge of criminal possession of a controlled substance, the district attorney has recommended the remedy of seventy hours' community service. Do you understand this?"

I peered over at my Lawyer for tacit guidance.

But he was deeply lost in his briefs just then.

I nodded yes.

"You understand," the judge continued, "that in so doing you waive your right to appeal in this matter. Even if you feel you were falsely arrested?"

False arrest? I thought to myself. *Was that an issue here?* I assumed I had been caught dead to rights—though I had tried to be as clandestine as one can be, buying a hit in the middle of Eighth Avenue during the peak of the Friday rush hour. *But had the police committed some breach of procedure?*

The judge was sharp.

She caught the look on my face.

"Do you feel you've had sufficient time to consult with your attorney?" she asked me.

Again I glanced over to him.

His head was out of his briefs now, and he was nodding yes so emphatically, I thought his spine was going to snap.

Community service it was.

There are a number of organizations that administer alternative-sentence programs. Cases operates strictly above 110th Street. My first day up there turned out to be interesting. Like every new arrival, I got the standard orientation spiel, designed to minimize the possibility of any friction with the surrounding community: No store runs or phone calls during work (you might walk into a police sweep operation where they arrest everyone within a certain area). No conversing with neighborhood people—especially man to woman (you might get into a beef with her old man; tales are told of guys eager to make a rep, showing up with a gun, ready to take out whoever dissed their woman). And of course no drugs or alcohol.

But what was interesting was what happened when we went off to work. We were driven to an empty lot where an abandoned building once stood. The structure had been demolished and all that was left was a huge mound of soil and debris in the rear of the property. Our task was to finish putting up a partially erected chain-link fence and move enough dirt to the front of the lot for fill.

In the van on the way over, the consensus among my co-offenders had been that since we were not getting paid for our labor it didn't make sense to work with any gusto.

"They ain't getting shit outta me" was the resolution. "I ain't bustin' my ass for nobody."

So for the longest time we stood around, reluctant workers, tossing all manner of obfuscation at the tasks at hand.

We debated tools:

We should have brought a posthole digger! How are we gonna plant poles without a posthole digger?

We debated process:

Won't we have to put another pole here? The whole damn thing'll collapse if you don't put'er up right.

We debated supplies:

These aren't the right hinges. We need different hinges for the gate.

Everybody seemed to be an expert on some aspect of the job and everybody felt their expertise was of greater value than their sweat. Eventually I got fed up with this routine and wandered toward the dirt mound, putting distance between me and the besieged supervisor. A few minutes later two other guys drifted over—a young, quiet brother sporting a fade haircut, boxer shorts sprouting out the top of his low-worn oversized black trousers like a bouquet; and a thin, light-skinned Spanish guy, dressed, for some inexplicable reason, as if he were out on a first date.

Out of sheer boredom I began spading dirt into a nearby wheelbarrow. The two of them stared on, bewildered. Self-starters were hardly appreciated or rewarded in this situation. Working hard didn't get you home any faster. And you wouldn't win any friends showing everyone else up with your enthusiasm.

But I didn't care about all that. All I wanted was for the day to be over with as quickly as possible. The way I saw it, time went by faster when you kept busy.

The dirt was hard and full of rocks, pieces of wood, and other fallout from the razed building. I worked slowly and methodically.

I wasn't out to bust my ass, I just wanted to keep busy. In a way this was my calling card. *I'm not out to earn a rep or kiss anybody's ass,* it said. *I'm here to do what I gotta do and go home. Whatever the rest of you want to do is your business.*

It wasn't long before the other two joined me. The young one first. He picked up a spade and began tentatively, poking at the soil here and there. Left to languish in his party clothes, the Spanish guy soon followed suit. After a while we fell into a fairly efficient rhythm; one loosening the dirt with a spade, one shoveling it into the wheel-barrow, and one ferrying the load to the front of the lot and dumping it. When any of us got bored with his task, he'd switch with another. Before long we were exchanging casual fragments of conversation. We had found, in the work, common ground.

Lunch break was upon us before we knew it. It was a quiet, serene afternoon. We all sat on the ground, in the shade thrown by the shadow of the building next door, and, just for that interlude, contented ourselves with the simple pleasure of eating.

"You a veteran?" the Spanish guy asked me out of the blue.

I told him no, I had missed Vietnam. But I believe I understood why the question had occurred to him. There must have been moments like this in Nam, brief refuge from the blood and guts, wherein men thrown together by grim circumstance huddled and ate in silence, each savoring, for a time, full possession of his own thoughts.

By the end of lunch, enough had been worked out about how

to proceed with the fence to determine that all hands would be needed. We stepped all over each other at first. But as quitting time grew near, we fell into a natural harmony and began working as a team: one of us cutting pipe, two of us hoisting chain link, one wiring it to the uprights, and so on. And out of our efforts something tangible emerged in steel and concrete.

We drew the attention of a few neighborhood kids, who watched our progress with the unconditional fascination children have for grown-ups caught doing grown-up things.

All it took was that one day and we were no longer just a rag-tag collection of druggies, winos, petty hustlers, panhandlers, and low-level dealers overseen by a hard-timer working off the terms of his parole. From then on, and for as long as we were bound together by order of the court, we were a unit. And by the end of each succeeding work day we knew something about one another that we hadn't known before.

I may be romanticizing things a bit. For sure there was plenty of thankless, finger-blistering, back-breaking work ahead. Like taming a weed-infested, rock-and-rubble-strewn wilderness of a lot into a habitable garden—a task more suited to tractors and backhoes than the rakes, spades, weed whackers, sweat, and spine we had at our disposal. All while a vicious pit bull next door threatened to break his leash and lock its jaws around someone's limbs.

But after my two and a half weeks at it, I can say for certain that there are a lot more positive things going on behind a hoe than behind the bars of a cell.

On my last day I am assigned to be one of the two people to accompany the supervisor to the Popeye's franchise for the day's food. As we wait for the order to be filled, I do a quick survey of what my seventy hours of work has accomplished. A building on one street has a fresh coat of waterproofing. Several gardens have been divested of weeds and debris and may now flourish. Needy residents who live near a community center in Washington Heights have a fresh store of USDA foodstuffs in their pantries, which we also helped to distribute. A ravaged shelter harboring the most desperate of the homeless got two days' worth of free cleaning service from us. A lady who brought us out cake as we worked in her yard now has her much-wanted personal garden bed. And in at least one city project, when children come to the playground each morning, they no longer have to trudge over beer cans, empty crack vials, and other litter of the night. All in all, I feel I have made amends.

As I step out of Popeye's, laden with two-piece chicken lunches, I find myself back where it all started, in front of a judge. Only this one is down from her perch, out of her robes, casting for votes in the heart of Harlem, and looking just a second away from panic.

"Hello, I'm Karen Burstein," she bravely intones, mistaking me for a local from the hood. "And I'm running for attorney general."

"Hi," I chirp back, brandishing a Popeye's box. "I'm Lee Stringer, I'm running for city council, and I'm giving out free fried chicken."

She laughs good naturedly.

I turn, disappear into the waiting van, poke my head out through the window, and give her a parting nod.

"That's the way you do it around here," I say.

Community Service, II. Harlem, 1994.

"Yo—Biggie Small!"

The voice is loud, intrusive.

"You can come and use my shower after work."

We are in The Van, heading toward The Site. There is the smell of a dozen or so boxed fried-chicken lunches obscenely commingling with that of an equal number of men and twice as many sneakers.

"Yo—Biggie Small!" he calls again.

The voice belongs to Reggie.

Reggie is a dark, compact, muscular guy. In his twenties, I'd say. He has the kind of explosive, restless energy that fares none too well in confined places. He has decided my name is Biggie Small. He's been at me ever since he got in the van.

Affable enough, but he's testing.

"Here, check this out," he says, revealing a tiny quantity of something he shouldn't have. "Take it and give me five dollars at the end of the week."

Of course he snatches it back as soon as I reach for it, and I curse myself for the lapse. I know that sooner or later this will come to a head. Sooner or later Reggie is going to try to "step to" me.

We pull up to a corner on West 118th Street, across from a junk-strewn vacant lot, half a block from a church, and within a block or two of where you can buy anything that can be bought on Harlem streets. There, behind a twelve-foot-high chain-link fence, sits a verdant oasis.

A community garden.

Grass lies evenly across the lot like a striking green, custom carpet. There are five columns of large garden boxes along the fence, fairly overflowing with carrots, watermelons, lettuce, corn, tomatoes; a veritable Caesar salad of produce. Flowers embellish the perimeter with bright bursts of color.

An oasis.

One by one we grunt our way out of the van, file through the gate, into the garden, and to the day's work. There are weeds to uproot, plants and lawn to be watered, paper and debris to be raked from the grounds and pulled from under the fencing. I spend the morning with a roller on a ten-foot extension pole. Using a special primer, I'm waterproofing the side of the building abutting the garden. All in all it's agreeable work. I'm left alone and I can work at my own pace.

We break for lunch at two o'clock. It is always fried chicken. The only consideration is whether you want it with "dirty rice" or fries. We joke about the predictability of the fare, but no one turns it down. Toiling under the sun builds an appetite.

After eating I settle down on a bench in the garden for a few minutes, when I hear footsteps behind me, squeaking across the sodden grass.

"Yo—Biggie Small! 'Sup?" cries Reggie.

He joins me on the bench.

It starts off as small talk.

"Say, man, you do dope?" he blurts.

"Nope."

"You shoot coke?"

"Nope."

"You like cut?"

"What?"

He leaps to his feet, spins around so that he's facing me.

There is a razor in his hand.

"I said do you like CUT, motherfucker!"

For a fraction of a second I can't take my eyes off the blade. I have to force my gaze upward. To his eyes.

"Wanna get cut?" he says. "Huh, motherfucker?"

I say and do nothing.

I go to zero.

Neither feeding nor resisting his actions.

"I ain't joking," he says, shifting his weight slightly.

The move is barely perceptible, but it registers with me.

I slide my eyes right to left. The place is eerily vacant. Everyone seems to have disappeared. I fight off a twitch of paranoia that tries to tell me some sort of plot is afoot. I rise slowly to my feet, my eyes locked on his. It's just a single-edge Gem blade. The kind you put in a razor. He is not all that close now either. He'd have to close in a step or two to use the thing.

I wait him out.

"Got any money on you?" he asks.

I shrug feebly. Palms up.

"Nope."

Standoff.

He has nowhere to go with this.

Only a few more seconds elapse before his shoulders slump and he pockets the razor. But it seems like forever to me.

Reggie screws a hasty aw-shucks grin in place.

"I was only kidding," he says.

I have been presented with Reggie's calling card, the price I pay for the earlier, eager weakness in the van. Confrontation is the currency of the pavement. If you want your space, you have to declare it in no uncertain terms. There are no rental agents on the sidewalk, and bullshit won't buy you much. I wonder if this is the end of it, or will he step to me again. I decide to stay real close to Reggie. For the rest of the day I'll be right on his ass.

After lunch they haul out a twenty-foot extension ladder and hand me a brush so I can get to the touchy spots at the top of the wall. I'm skeptical about the wet grass. I've had a ladder go out from under me before and it was only by a miracle that I didn't get hurt. But I keep my mouth shut and proceed, cautiously, up the first few rungs. Halfway up I hear the supervisor call out.

"Someone get over here and hold this ladder for him."

I hear the shuffle of feet approaching the ladder, feel a steadying hand grip the lower rungs.

"Yo—Biggie Small!" comes the voice again.

I angle myself sideways and peer down at Reggie. His head is cocked backward. He's grinning up at me. I only hesitate for a second. But in that instant it becomes clear to me, somehow, that I can trust him down there.

Up the ladder I go.

8

Hell's Kitchen, Fall 1994. It's one of those bright, glorious Indian-summer days, gold dust streaming through the front windows of the *Street News* editorial office, the treetops across Ninth Avenue swaying gently in the breeze. I'm standing hunched over my desk, teeth clenched, cursing and muttering at the printer—one of those worthless, low-end Panasonic dot-matrix jobs with a temperament all its own—sitting in frozen silence, red "error" light blinking dumbly back at me, refusing to print so much as a digit. And what keeps running through my mind is, *Why am I doing this?*

But I know why.

I did it to myself.

I went and got myself an honest job.

Not that I was looking. I had an income. I sold papers. As many and for as long as my needs required. I didn't really feel I was missing anything out of life by being on the street either—at least not anything that could be had by a paycheck. And I wasn't really interested in being employed simply for the sake of it. What I wanted was to do something worth a bit of satisfaction as well as a buck. Something that might make a difference.

Writing for *Street News* seemed like it might be the ticket. For three years its circulation had been dwindling, a situation I attributed to its languishing content—twenty-four pages of lackluster filler interspersed with the intolerant, misanthropic posturing of Ayn Rand-objectivist editor-in-chief John Connolly, the hand-picked successor of founder Hutchinson Persons. Connolly had just been shown the door, and a movement was afoot to dip down into the streets for new editorial people. I imagined that as a writer I might help light up *Street News'* pages and that this might help it emerge from its doldrums.

I was wrong, of course.

It turned out there were are all sorts of forces working against *Street News* beyond the remedy of lively prose and a sharp blue pencil. But not knowing this at the time, I was full of passion, and I suppose that this—coupled with the fact that I was the genuine article, a living, breathing creature of the streets—got me the job.

That and my willingness to work for peanuts.

It also got me a place to crash.

Officially this wasn't part of the bargain. *Street News* enjoyed its rent-free floor-through loft space on Ninth Avenue by virtue of the generosity of Seymour Durst, patriarch of one of New York's largest real estate empires. I'm sure it wasn't in his plans that I set up residence in his building. But there was a small yet sleep-worthy couch in the office, and I did find myself working late nights, and it was not entirely unheard of for an employee to crash at the office after a long, hard day's work. All I had to do was make sure I was up and about before anyone else arrived each morning so that the rest of the staff were none the wiser as to where I laid my head.

So here I am, living at and working for *Street News*.

What I do mostly is write.

Besides doing features, I do three regular columns: "Graffiti," a sampling of brief, perky items that appear just inside the front cover as a sort of instant reward for opening the paper; "Tales from the Rails," humorous reportage on subway experiences; and "Ask Homey," a Q&A section inside the back cover in which I respond to readers' questions about homeless people and life on the streets.

I have myself to blame for this too. I instigated these columns with my head filled with thoughts of *Street News'* glorious turnaround. And, since ideas die a quick death but for the doing, it fell on me— ours being a small operation—to carry them out.

Not that I'm complaining exactly. I enjoy working with words. That part of the job delivers a certain satisfaction. But as for any of my work making a real difference in the larger scheme of things, as for it having any impact on the growing public resentment toward homeless people, for example, I have had to climb down from that high horse. There are just too many fierce and strident voices out there these days, milking events for the short term, pushing the shortsighted notion that circling the wagons is in everyone's interest. And they all seem to speak louder than me.

So, despite my once-hearty expectations, I've come to face the fact, inch by frustrating inch, that writing for *Street News* is just another job after all. And I'm three flights above Ninth Avenue, boxed off from the sweetness of the day, going ballistic over an errant Panasonic, and wondering what I'm doing here, when the phone starts ringing.

I pick it up and it's some gravel-voiced coot—Paul Ischi "with an *i*," he says—who right off the bat starts drooling shmooze into my ear, carrying on about what a *big* fan of *Street News* he is, how he *always* buys a copy when he sees it, and what a *great* job we're doing, and so on. Only, he picked the wrong day to try to stroke this malcontent.

I'm pissed off at the printer.

I'm pissed off at the entire Panasonic Corporation.

I'm pissed off at my whole miserable, misspent blunder of a life.

"What's on your mind, Mr. Ischi with an *i*?" I ask.

He tells me—in no uncertain terms, mind you—that he wants *Street News* to do a story about his homeless organization, Shepherd of the Streets, preferably on the front page, and if it could be in the next issue, he'd be happy about that too.

Well, I'm in just the right mood to straighten him out on that one.

"We may not be The New York Times here," I huff, "but we're not the corner deli either. You can't just call up and order a cover story like a salami sandwich."

This seems to slow him down at least. He apologizes for being out of line and confesses ignorance about how newspapers work.

"Perhaps I should speak to your editor," he says.

Only my editor-in-chief is at home, about to give birth to a curly-haired, blue-eyed baby boy. It's just me and our Gal Friday, Barbara, a good-natured, raven-haired Greek who has somehow appropriated Loni Anderson's face and figure. She's at the next desk, merrily typing the morning away on her own, perfectly functioning computer.

"You're talking to the *senior* editor," I take pains in letting this Ischi fellow know. "And I can tell you right now you're off on the wrong foot. Who or what goes on our cover is strictly an editorial decision, and that's based on the merits of the story as we determine it."

That's the way it starts once you've nailed down an honest job. All of a sudden you become self-important and find yourself regurgitating pompous blather like this bit about fifth-estate imperatives.

"Why don't we start over again," I suggest. "Do you think you can give me the Shepherd of the Streets story in twenty-five words or less?"

"Well, I was inspired by something Aristotle said," he replies, slinging a little pomposity of his own. "'If you want wisdom,' Aristotle said, 'go amongst the people.' So I decided to come to New York and that's what I'd do. I always wanted to live in New York.

"I slept on park benches, in doorways, even in a shelter once. And the most important thing I learned from living on the street is compassion for homeless people. Nobody listens to them. That's why they talk to me. Because I'm the only one who listens to them. But I wanted to do more than listen. And I decided to make it official, with Shepherd of the Streets, Inc. I thought *Street News* might want an exclusive."

It's hardly the stuff of *Eyewitness News*. But it's not as if we have an AP wire on the premises either. I figure we might get some mileage out of the grass-roots angle—the idea of helping people one-on-one on the streets. I'm thinking maybe a miniprofile, three, four hundred words or so, an on-the-scene photo or two, something Barbara can write up. Barbara's not a staff writer, but was pressed into service on a previous light piece.

"I'll be frank with you, Mr. Ischi," I tell him. "I don't see this as a cover story. But we're always interested in people who work with the homeless. I'm going to put someone on the phone to talk with you."

Barbara gets on the phone, pulls out a pad and a pen, and starts uh-huhing into the receiver. I go back to wrestling with the Panasonic. Before you know it, I forget all about Paul Ischi and Shepherd of the Streets.

But a week later he calls back, sniffing around for his story, wondering when it will run. I ask Barbara about it and she whips up a page and a half of cute, sweet, and fluffy copy.

Only I hate cute and sweet.

And I'll chew ground glass before I put up with fluffy.

"Little thin for a profile," I tell her. "Could use some meat, don't you think? Didn't you get any background stuff? Who he is? Where he's from? That sort of thing?"

"Not really," she says. "He doesn't like to talk about himself. Says he doesn't want the story to be about him, he wants it to be about Shepherd of the Streets."

I tell you, the guy just seemed to have a knack for ticking me off.

"Well, if he's so picky," I say, "why doesn't he write the damn thing himself? And while he's at it, he can print up twenty thousand copies, get on the subway, and peddle them too."

As she always does when I spout off like this, Barbara remains mute, knowing the storm will pass.

"Look," I tell her more calmly. "We're *Street News*, and this story's about the homeless. That's our bread and butter. If anything, we should really sell this thing. Give it some oomph."

What Barbara does is offer to call Ischi back. Only she wants me to write down what questions she should ask, which won't work because it's really a play-it-by-ear thing, and Barbara doesn't really have a reporter's instincts.

Not that I'm anybody's Mike Wallace either.

I can write, but as I've come to realize, newspapers aren't really a writer's medium. You do have to be able to write, of course, and preferably with a certain craft and economy. But it's the immediacy of the story you're covering that earns you ink, not the profundity of your prose—more a matter of the gossip's ear than the poet's muse.

Newspapers are more concerned with the details of man's business than the progress of his soul. For that it needs reporters. And what reporters do is break stories.

I hadn't broken much of anything in the two years I've been at it except an old IBM-clone computer.

"Tell you what, Barbara," I suggest. "Why don't we invite Ischi up here and we'll both interview him. Then you can rewrite the story. How about that?"

Barbara says fine—she really is an agreeable sort. I call up Ischi, set up the interview for the next day, and promptly banish him from my mind once again. So I'm hardly prepared for what I see when the downstairs buzzer sounds the next afternoon. Ischi comes huffing up the stairs draped shoulder-to-floor in a pleated ink-black robe, a wide, black satin sash girdled around his middle, a huge Byzantine cross dangling from a chain—competing for space on his chest with a longish salt-and-pepper beard—and something resembling an inverted top hat perched precariously atop his head. Old, gray, and bent, he looks to me like the Grim Reaper, come to harvest a few souls.

"So this is it," he says, standing just inside the door eyeballing our humbly appointed office. "*Street News.*"

"Forgive me, uh, father," I blurt, wondering, *What is he? Priest? Bishop? Monk?* "I had no idea you were a, ah—of the cloth."

"You're the fellow I spoke to on the phone, aren't you?" he says, lumbering closer, his tired gray eyes giving me the once-over. "We kinda got off on the wrong foot there for a minute, didn't we."

"I suppose we did," I confess, waiting for the wrath of God to strike me dead. "I believe you also spoke to Barbara here," I add quickly, offering her up like a sacrifice. "She's going to sit in with us."

"Great," he chirps. "Two heads are better than one."

We get down to it and I find myself tiptoeing around the religion thing. What I know on the subject can be etched on a flea's navel with room left over for the Lord's Prayer and the Dead Sea Scrolls.

"So you're a priest?" I say.

"Monk, abbot," he says. "Same thing. That's just what they call it in the Orthodox church."

"What church were you with?" I ask

"Saint German of Alaska," he says.

"You came all the way here from Alaska?" I ask him.

"Long Island," he says. "Alaska's just the name of the Church. It's Greek Orthodox."

"Oh, so you are Greek," I try. "Barbara here's Greek too."

"No, I'm Hungarian," Ischi says, and explains to me that Orthodox churches are all of the same doctrine regardless of their ethnic distinctions.

I was starting to get a headache.

"We can sort all that out later," I tell him. "We can call the Church for the background stuff."

"Oh, but I left the Church," Ischi quickly points out, "when I decided to come here and live amongst the people. I'm not involved with them anymore and I'd like to respect their privacy."

I wonder why, then, the Holy Roller drag?

"I'm still a priest," he explains. "Once you're ordained in the Orthodox church, you're ordained for life."

"Sort of like Mayor Koch," I throw in.

That gets a chuckle out of him.

"I had a good thirty years with the Church," he says. "But now I want to do more."

"And you felt you could be more effective on the streets," Barbara chimes in. A statement more than a question.

"Oh, the Church does a good enough job when they do it," Ischi says, drawing in a world-weary lungful. "But it's only ten percent of what they could be doing."

I can see his point. In my nocturnal wanderings I've certainly walked by enough big churches with their doors gated up for the night and homeless people sleeping outside on the steps. Something is definitely wrong with that picture.

I mention this to Ischi and he launches into a wholesale indictment of various and sundry bureaucracies that I find a bit strong in tone for a man once hewn to the cloistered life. And when he declares that "God Himself" couldn't get in to see Archbishop Iakova without an appointment two weeks in advance, I pick up on the resentment lurking behind the kindly, philosophical self-sacrificing soul he has thus far made himself out to be.

"So you and this Iakova had your differences, then," I say. "Did you feel the church was holding you back as a priest? That might make an interesting angle for the story."

"Please," Ischi says softly, his hand up in a vague "stop" gesture. "It's not me that's important. I'd rather this be about the organization and the work it's doing."

"Tell us about the work Shepherd of the Streets is doing," I purr.

He talks us through about two dozen eight-by-tens he has brought along; him standing solemn, stiff, and berobed in the middle of each one, flanked by a small cluster of faceless, anonymous people, all gaping blankly into the camera. You can go through all twenty of them and not gain the slightest clue as to what they are about. The only curiosity is the smiling, fresh-faced pup idling in the corner of about half of them, looking somewhat out of place.

"I met him in the park," Ischi says. "A very nice young fellow. He volunteered to help me with my work."

I peer over Ischi's shoulder to get a closer gander at this baby-faced Samaritan.

"Doesn't he look like Tom Cruise?" Ischi says, gazing fondly at his young ward.

"You a fan of Tom Cruise?" I ask.

"Oh, yes," he says, eyes firing up. "Wonderful actor."

"Tell me about some of the other street people you've met as shepherd of the streets," I find myself asking. Ischi settles back in his chair and, with a certain relish, serves up a rogue's gallery of the lost: an HIV-positive hooker still pulling tricks; a near-dead doper, desperately seeking treatment but sandbagged by the system; a terminally ill HRA ward who's been cut off from his benefits; there's even a young, angry immigrant who confessed to Ischi that he murdered someone in cold blood and got away with it. Like a feed-the-starving-children pitchman, Ischi sums this all up with an appeal to the kindness of strangers.

"So what we're looking for at this time," he says, "is the gift of a building. So that we may continue our work."

I thank him for coming, and he groans his way out of the chair and slowly makes for the door, tossing off homespun homilies all the way. When he is gone, Barbara and I find ourselves immersed in sudden stillness, hoisting eyebrows at each other.

"So what'd you think?" I ask her.

She shrugs and says Ischi seemed like a nice enough guy to her. I agree, but I have two main reservations, the first being his story. Though I would like to think there are all-sacrificing men among us, Ischi didn't make me a believer. The thought of him, at his advanced age, trading in his sheltered, comfortable suburban priesthood for a bench in Central Park just didn't wash.

He was no Mother Teresa, he was a Tom Cruise fan.

That was the other thing that bothered me.

"It's your story," I tell Barbara. "But I think it'd be a good idea to get in touch with that church in Long Island and see if they know him."

"Why?" she says. "You think he might be a phony?"

"Nothing specific," I tell her. "But that bit about needing a building makes it a different ball game. If we're going to give him a crack at hitting our readers up for donations, then we owe it to them to check him out."

"I can just leave that part out," she says. "—About the building."

"Yeah, but if he's legit, it would do *Street News* well to be instrumental in his getting what he needs. And anyway, I would think you'd like to know if he's trying to get one over on us, for your own sake."

"I suppose you're right," Barbara says. "But I'm not really good at that sort of thing. I tend to trust people too much."

Hearing Barbara use the words *trust* and *too much* in the same sentence stirs up a peculiar pang in my gut. I tell her to do her best and she goes to it. I go back to my own writing, but find myself peering over at Barbara—scribbling on a notepad, phone propped against her ear—and I can't help wondering, with a twinge of envy, what had so graced the course of her life that at thirty-odd years old she is still capable of trusting "too much." And when she finishes on the phone and reports to me that Ischi was indeed what he claimed, abbot of St. German, and for eighteen years to boot, I can see it is a happy victory for her. One that gives the fact that I do not let it go at that a somewhat brutish cast.

"Ischi said he'd been in the Church for thirty years," I tell her. "What about those other twelve years?"

"I suppose I could call them back," she offers, the sunshine in her face clouding over. "Maybe they can tell me."

"Now you're thinking like a reporter," I tell her brightly. "And if they say they don't know, have them tell you who would."

Over the next two days Barbara has a phone growing out of her ear. Lead by lead, she furrows her way all the way back to 1965, when Ischi began his illustrious career as an Episcopalian priest in Philadelphia. From there he became something of a Renaissance man, hopscotching across the Orthodox church's multiethnic terrain in one Russian, then Romanian, then Bulgarian, then Greek, parish after another, culminating in his eighteen-year stint at St. German.

Behind him he left a paper trail—in the form a series of memos to and from the diocese—of which we were able to get faxed copies. What they revealed was that as far back as the seventies Ischi had become something of a pariah among his fellow clergy. In "recommending" him for transfer to other parishes, his superiors expressed their displeasure with his "falling short of the solemn ordination oath," whatever that meant, and his failure to "obey your bishop and the canons of the Church."

Before packing him off to St. German in 1977, the New York Diocese of the Bulgarian Orthodox Church concluded Ischi was "uncomfortable among us, our people, and our traditions."

In addition to this material, Barbara manages to rustle up three people who knew "Father Paul" personally, all of whom declared that they didn't quite approve of his "methods." None of them will cop to anything more specific than that they found him "too controversial"—about what they won't say. And all of them refuse to be quoted on the record.

It is obvious to me from all this that Ischi's leaving the Church had less to do with Aristotle than with incompatibility. But what I want to know is, if Ischi and the Church were at odds from so far back, why did it take him twenty years to get the sudden urge to step off? And if Ischi's failure as a priest was what the Church meant by his being too controversial, why do they release this information to us now that he is finally off their hands?

On a hunch I decide to speak with the diocese myself, and call their press office. The phone is answered in a purring voice, which I take to belong to the press liaison. He certainly remembers Ischi.

"It's my understanding he wasn't happy with the Church, and left the priesthood," he is quick to point out.

"I'm aware of that," I say. "But I understand he got himself entangled in some kind of controversy just before he left."

"That was over two years ago," he says. "I don't see any point in bringing all that up again."

"Do you remember what all the fuss was about?" I want to know.

"I'm sure I couldn't say," he replies. "It didn't really involve the

Church. There's really nothing more I can tell you."

But he has already told me plenty.

When I hang up, Barbara is peering at me, *Well...?* written all over her face.

"I just got off the phone with the diocese press office," I tell her. "And when I mentioned the word *controversy*, they said they weren't going to get into all that *again*."

"Uh-huh," Barbara says, waiting for more.

"Well, what does that tell you?"

"That they've been through it before, I guess." she says on cue.

"Exactly," the pedant in me says. "You're sounding more like a reporter every minute. "Now, if their *press office* was involved, it means that whatever Ischi did to embarrass them must have attracted someone in the press. And if I were you, I'd see what kind of local rags they have out there in Long Island, and call their morgues. See if the name Ischi rings any bells."

It takes a little doing, but Barbara tracks down three local papers in Long Island, one of which—a broadsheet named *Three Village Herald*—covers Setauket. The guy in their morgue comes up with a few items from over two years back involving a William Vaughn Ischie, spelled with an *e* at the end.

"Close enough," I tell her. "See if you can get them to fax us anything they have on him. Tell them we'll give them credit for whatever we use."

For the rest of the day my eyes keep flying to the fax machine. But Barbara seems oblivious. She's quieter than usual, in fact. In light of the week's events, I find that curious.

It isn't until late the next afternoon that the faxes come in. I see them hanging from the machine when I return from lunch; three articles, all of them about a William Vaughn Ischie, president of two real estate holding companies, in which capacity he was investigated by the IRS for tax fraud, indicted by none other than former prosecutor Rudolph Giuliani's office, for which charge he eventually wound up behind bars.

Soon after he was released from prison, our "Paul Ischi" landed homeless and penniless on the streets of New York City and began his two-year odyssey "amongst the people."

This, of course, is no coincidence.

William Vaughn Ischie and Father Paul Ischi are the same man.

Nor is it a coincidence that Shepherd of the Streets is in dire need of a building. For without it he cannot once again ply the scheme by which he had manipulated over four million dollars' worth of donated real estate while under the nonprofit, tax-free patronage of the Orthodox church.

The play was simple: He ran classified ads in local newspapers on behalf of the Church, soliciting gifts of "distressed" and/or "hard to sell" buildings from realtors and corporations. When he got the properties, he would sell them to himself for a dollar—through his real estate holding companies—and then quickly liquidate them for whatever hard cash he could get.

Most of the properties were lemons and couldn't fetch much on the open market. But Ischie made up for this in volume, trading over a hundred parcels during the time the scheme was in operation. The key factor in his ability to obtain this high volume was that through his associate, appraiser William Blackmore, he was able to offer donors a sweeter-than-usual deal. Blackmore assessed all the donated properties at full market value, despite the fact that they were routinely run-down and uninhabitable, thus providing an under-the-table tax bonus so compelling it even attracted the likes of mega-realtor Harry Helmsley and Eli Lilly Corporation, the pharmaceutical giant.

It also attracted the scrutiny of the IRS, which couldn't quite reconcile the high valuation at which the properties were written off with the bargain-basement prices they actually fetched when liquidated by Ischie.

After their investigation, Ischie and Blackmore were indicted for conspiracy to commit tax fraud. Both copped a plea. Blackmore lost his license and served an undisclosed sentence, later disappearing upstate, where he has remained incommunicado ever since. Ischie was able to use his age and association with the Church to good advantage in negotiating a sentence of six months in a minimum-security facility and a nominal $150 fine.

Now paroled, defrocked, and stripped of all worldly possessions, here Ischi was, evidently preparing to run the whole scheme once again with *Street News* standing in for the classifieds. *Street News* may not be known for its outstanding journalism, I tell myself, but when push comes to shove, we can do the job. Ischie would get his story all right. But not the quaint little promo he was seeking. And for the lion's share of the grunt work, credit is due to Barbara Bales.

"Thanks to your work," I tell her, "*Street News* has its first genuine breaking story since they started publishing this miserable rag."

But it's not pride I see on Barbara's face.

Only more clouds.

"This is really not my cup of tea," she says, twiddling a pencil between her small pale fingers. "They're really going to be pissed off. What if they come after me?"

Barbara was originally hired to work in the *Street News* distribution center, wholesaling the paper to the vendors. Being a reporter was never among her ambitions, and now it dawns on me that encouraging her to make a practice of doubt has not necessarily been the great gift I smugly assumed it would be. Doubt, by nature, paves the way to fear.

"So I'll take the heat for you," I tell her. "I'll write it up and put my byline on it."

"I wish you would," she says.

It isn't for the sake of chivalry, my offer. The fact is, I got quite a rush from tracking down Ischi's secret. And having had a taste of the hunt, I am primed and eager to confront him, to move in for the kill. *So this is what it feels like to be a real reporter,* I'm thinking. And when I do get Ischi on the phone, self-importance is flowing through me like a drug.

"You made one mistake," I tell him, unable to resist treating myself to at least one gloat. "You underestimated *Street News.* You should have stuck to the classifieds."

"The hell with *Street News,*" he barks, dropping all priestly pretense. "Nobody reads your bullshit paper anyway. If you want to speak to me, speak to my lawyer."

His lawyer—later joined by his PR man, a young, third-tier grunt trying to make his bones in a large firm—does his pro bono best to paint a picture of Ischi as the fall guy, caught between an unscrupulous appraiser and powerful corporate interests. But by then I have found out that the cofounder of Shepherd of the Streets is none other than Sonny Bloch, a smarmy, Reagan-era huckster who preaches the gospel of wealth-through-real-estate on WOR radio. With this green-hungry piece of work involved, I know it isn't just for the sake of the down-and-out that they're seeking a bit of New York City real estate.

When I sit down to write the story, I have an embarrassment of riches as far as angles are concerned; Ischi the hoodlum priest, Giuliani the star prosecutor, Bloch the radio celebrity, and Helmsley the real estate king, all entwined in a minor detective story with Dashiell

Hammett possibilities. I am overwhelmed by it at first, unable to whip it all into a brisk narrative.

After three oblique and muddled drafts, I finally noodle out the essence of the story, but I have to race against the clock to make deadline, feverishly tapping it out on Barbara's computer late into the evening while they stand by at the printing plant, waiting for me to fax it down.

It is as close to a "Hold the presses!" finish as I will ever get. And in the heat of the moment I even imagine that the *Post* or the *News* might pick the story up and that *Street News* might at last be put on the map as a *real* newspaper.

But the story raises not a whisper.

Street News just isn't a big enough stick to stir up any significant ruckus. There is no particular peak in circulation. We don't get any sudden calls from the dailies asking for details, and *Street News* continues to lose money.

Barbara is laid off a few months later due to budget cuts. She is hired by another newspaper, but is soon let go for her lack of "initiative." I stay on, having gotten used to sleeping indoors, even after there is no more money for salaries. But nobody rushes up to anoint me into the brotherhood of *real* newspapermen.

It is just as well.

For me it isn't an altogether healthy thing that my suspicions were borne out, that there *was* something there after all. Because, when you get right down to it, in an imperfect world such as ours, there is always something there. And had my cynicism been validated by any public glory, I might be out there this very moment, thoroughly addicted to the business of dredging up somebody else's muck—not the most constructive reason to climb out of bed in the morning.

So it is just as well the story didn't make a big splash.

I squander enough spirit puffing on a crack pipe.

Two years after my story, Sonny Bloch gets himself indicted for real estate fraud. It is in all the papers. And shortly after that I pick up a copy of the *Spirit* and spot an item that confirms my suspicions regarding Ischi, the Tom Cruise fan, that I had kept to myself. He has been arrested, the *Spirit* reports, for attempting to solicit sex from a teenage boy.

112

9

Valentine's adoptive father, Richard, imagined himself something of a poet, seeking victory over the streets in words. Not too far in the past, he had also imagined himself something of a benevolent pimp. But that's another story.

When I met Richard, he was, like me, just another urban vagabond, peddling *Street News* to passersby. He hailed from Jersey originally. What town, I don't recall. But it must have been some kind of dysfunctional hellhole. Because every tale he tells of his past is fraught with cruel and unusual tribulations.

Resentful, loveless parentage.

Suspicious and angry neighbors.

Cold, unrelenting institutions.

The kind of repressed and lost little burg that squeezes the life out of you.

By the time he landed in New York, even his humble home-and-hearth ambitions—marriage, career, home, family—had been all but crushed to dust. He'll tell you the story at the drop of a hat: the treachery of his ex-wife, to whom he had proposed even though he knew she was already pregnant by another man. The hostility of his ex-in-laws, who presumed him to be the deflowerer of their daughter. The bureaucracy of the system, which granted to his ex-wife most of the spoils of their failed union. He'll tell you how they all conspired to upend his lot.

From then on it was strictly working girls for Richard. When they hit you below the belt, it was mainly your wallet that took the blow. He came to New York with one ace in the hole, the by-product of a failed attempt on his life. A Jersey pimp, who took exception to Richard's doting sponsorship of one of his working girls, made a determined try at vehicular homicide, but only succeeded in adding several bones to the list of broken things in Richard's life. And Richard had the wherewithal to commit the number on the offending license plate to memory and get himself a hungry lawyer. After that it was just a matter of time—and the application of a little jurisprudence— before all the pain and anguish he had suffered lying half conscious in the middle of a Jersey street would pay off big-time in a Jersey civil court.

Richard also had the good sense to relocate to this side of the Jersey line while waiting on the slow-grinding wheels of Justice, content to mope through his intervening indigence among the homeless on the streets of New York City, hobbling around on crutches, sleeping in homeless shelters, eating in soup kitchens, and selling *Street News* here and there. But old habits die hard, and Richard spent a considerable portion of his time communing with the ladies of the night who trod the pavement along Tenth Avenue, never quite the john yet ever the wannabe lover.

To look at Richard—T-shirt and blue jeans, hair down to his shoulders, with a red bandanna wrapped pirate style around his head— you might mistake him for a hippie. But he came off more like an urban redneck, though he lacked the conviction, which, to me, being black, was his saving grace. He did have the requisite worship of firearms, though. He would quite literally quote lock, stock, and barrel about them. More than once I heard him spout off about how he'd like to take his "thirty-aught-six," or whatever, and equalize this or that situation. But my reading of him was that if it came to squeezing off rounds at someone, Richard wouldn't really be there.

That was the sad thing about all his gruff posturing. Like most of us, all Richard really wanted was a bit of honest fellowship and an easier time of it. And like most of us, he just couldn't quite get a handle on how. So his life has been one long, sad litany of unrequited loves, misdirected longings, and misplaced loyalties, all of which the poet in him has set to rhyme, amassing a treasure trove of past laments that he keeps in Jersey, locked away in a trunk.

When Richard's windfall comes in, he installs himself in a one-bedroom sublet just a few blocks from *Street News'* editorial office, where I have nudged my way in as senior editor—the title being in lieu of any decent money. And since Richard presumes that in winning my favor he will come to see his poems in print, this is when I get to know him. He appears regularly at the door, coffee and doughnuts in hand.

"Breakfast is on me," he says.

And sometimes lunch or dinner too.

He also feeds me schemes—unwieldy and half-baked ones designed to put *Street News* on the map once and for all. I give them a polite ear, poke at the holes here and there. But unlike some among his newfound circle of friends, I won't juice his ego for a shot at his cash. I do hit him up for emergency loans now and then, which, to preserve my line of credit, I take special pains to repay.

But mostly it is restlessness that has Richard dabbling in *Street News'* business. His sudden liquidity has not had the impact on his life he thought it would. It has not made him the man of substance he longs to be. This is New York City after all. And a poor fellow has to actually get his hands on eighty grand or so, as Richard has, before he realizes that it isn't what they call *real* money at all. It's certainly not enough to buy him grand entree into the ranks of the high-and-mighty. Which leaves Richard dangling among us smaller fish, where a wad on your hip gets a more wide-eyed reception.

He becomes a Big-Time Charlie at the soup kitchens, where he sometimes appears to rescue souls from their handout meal, whisking them off to the nearest greasy spoon. And when he strolls along Tenth Avenue at night, he spreads a few tens and twenties among the working girls in consideration of their hard-luck stories,

TOWER BOOKS—SUNRISE
7840 Macy Plaza Drive
Citrus Heights, CA 95610
(916) 961 - 7202
51871 Reg 1 4:39 pm 01/03/00


```
S GRAND CENTRAL WIN   1 @ 12.95      12.95
SUBTOTAL                             12.95
TAX: State - 6.25%                     .81
TAX: City - 1.5%                       .19
TOTAL SALES TAX                       1.00
TOTAL                                13.95
CREDIT SLIP REDEEMED                 15.07
CHANGE                                1.12
```

Exchanges/Defective Returns
May be made within 14 DAYS
With ORIGINAL RECEIPT.
IDENTIFICATION may be required.
THANK YOU FOR SHOPPING AT TOWER BOOKS.

and by and by he earns himself a little status and deference among the lost. It is through this kind of restless wandering that Richard comes to meet Valentine's mother, Suzi.

Suzi is a past-due tourist, a Brazilian national who came to visit the Apple and long overstayed the welcome her visa provided. But if New York loves anything, it's displaced young foxes of little material means. There is always room amid the costume-jewel glitter of the Times Square area for one more diamond in the rough. Especially one with Suzi's spunk, figure, and vaguely foreign intrigue. She has little problem finding fast money off the books. But as is often the case in the business of twilight amusements, fresh meat travels along an inverse track—starting at "the top," as it were, and working its way down from there—and Suzi's descent has been as quick and sure as any.

Exotic dancer.

Peepshow queen.

Escort.

Hooker.

Skeezer.

At the bottom of it all she finds herself left with little more than the clothes on her back, two kinds of drug habits, and little baby Valentine kicking in her belly.

Did I say old habits die hard?

When Richard spots Suzi, sitting at a soup kitchen table, belly out to here, a mangy black crackhead excuse for a pimp at her side, he sees another damsel in distress—a train by which he had certainly been hit before—and anticipating that her gratitude and his solvency might win for him what his want of looks and charm might not, he once again plays the white knight. With a quick flash of his cash, he makes the same vow to Suzi that he had once before made so disastrously.

"You don't have to sell yourself on the street for that crackhead," he tells her. "Come, you can live with me. Have your baby and I'll give it my name."

All Suzi has to do is say yes.

A few months later, in the middle of February, one day shy of the holiday that bears her name, Valentine is born. And within a matter of weeks Richard is brandishing her to everyone he knows, a tiny, vague bundle of wailing pinkness nestled in a blanket. Hairless, elliptical head; dark black eyes; chubby, piggly-wiggly fingers and toes; and a huge, distended naval.

She's a regular piss factory, too

And Richard, proud papa that he is, industrial-size box of Pampers crammed into his knapsack, worships every golden drop that comes out of her. He can hardly wait to get to the business of changing her tiny dirty drawers. Talk about being smitten! Rarely does Richard appear in public without little Valentine dangling from a harness lashed to his chest. He cannot pass a store without investigating whether there is anything at all inside for his little girl. And oh how cute the working girls think she is! For that brief first blush of parenthood Richard is a man that has it all—his woman, child, home, and the better part of $80,000 in the bank.

I was rooting for him. Who doesn't want to believe that if money can't buy happiness outright, it can at least pave the way? Only Valentine's mama is not down with the domestic-bliss scene. Richard's homey heaven is her landlocked hell. She is far too young to be pinned down by motherhood, and Richard has offered little else—no courtship to speak of, no giddy nights out on the town, no circle of friends to socialize with—nothing to compete with her passion for the streets. He has simply acquired her, in a kind of distress sale, and installed her, complete with child, in his home.

It becomes a conflict of compulsions really. Suzi is restless. The twilight of the street life calls to her. But Richard wants her for his own. All Suzi wants is to scurry back to her cocaine buzz, and all Richard wants—other than brandishing Valentine to the world—is to bury his face in her pubic fuzz.

And Suzi knows just how to play that one.

It's "no dollee, no tickee" all the way, and she certainly knows her way to the door.

Pretty soon Richard is mother, father, housekeeper, and john, and Suzi is off on an endless roller-coaster run, beaming up and sniffing back down with a vengeance.

Methadone for breakfast.

Crack for lunch.

Dope for dinner.

And dealer's choice at night.

Richard finds himself shelling out a couple hundred a day for Suzi's buzz. But even then, between the twitching, the jonesing, and the nodding, he can hardly get a tongue in edgewise.

"At this rate," he confides to me—and any other willing ear— "I'll be broke in a year."

"So why do you give her the money?" I ask, even though, druggie that I am, I envy Suzi's easy endowment.

"I tell her no," he says, "but she starts smashing things. I'm afraid she'll hurt the child."

The child.

She has become the lever by which Richard seeks to move the world his way. For the sake of the child Suzi should be the sober, loving mother, wife, and companion he yearns for so badly.

"If you're concerned about Valentine's safety," I tell him, "why don't you call the police?"

"If I do," he says, "and they find out about Suzi's drugging, they might take Valentine away."

"Maybe that's better," I tell him. "For Valentine's sake—until you can get Suzi straightened out."

But I can see his wheels turning, contemplating that empty bed, thinking even a fraction of a loaf is better than none at all.

"Oh, sure," he says. "They'd love that. Child Services would love to get their hands on a nice white baby."

Richard imagines that the city hungers and thirsts after fresh children. And that white ones are the most prized of all.

"Richard," I tell him, "I have seen you be mother and father to that child. You dote on her. She doesn't want for a thing. Anyone can see that you love her. Nobody's going to take Valentine away."

"Yeah, but I got an open warrant back in Jersey," he confides. "A marijuana-possession charge, and I never went to court. If Child Services does a background check on me, I'm screwed."

This is how it has gone every time I see Richard, him constantly and openly lamenting his misery, even while steadfastly refusing any reasonable out.

"And if they haul me off to jail in Jersey," he says, "who'll take care of Valentine?"

A few months later Richard strides in the door as if he's just won the lottery.

"Well, I'm going to do it," he beams. "I'm going to make Suzi an honest woman." He actually says that. "We're going to tie the knot."

I can't help myself. The only reaction that comes out of me is to earnestly ask him if he has gone completely insane. Quietly and patiently at first, and eventually at full rant, I throw reason after reason why marrying Suzi will only buy him more pain.

But he has come armed with reasons of his own.

Too many for them all to be sincere.

"It will give the child a legal name," he says.

"It will make Suzi a citizen," he says.

"It will give me legal custody of Valentine," he says.

"I'll be able to claim them on my SSI disability," he says.

"Besides"—he finally grins, and this is what's really at the bottom of it—"once Suzi's married to me, I have certain rights. She won't be able to tell me no."

That confirms it for me.

Richard has indeed gone mad. And after five hours of pleading, bullying, sarcasm, interrogation, and reasoning, I have not brought him a whit closer to sanity. Nail him on one point and he slides over to another.

We are a dog. Me, the head, chasing him, the tail.

The nuptials are conducted the next day in a tiny, dusty courtroom in Chinatown, the "happy couple" decked out in T-shirts and jeans, Valentine restless and squirming all the while. In all of twenty minutes it's a done deal. The "wedding party" convenes immediately thereafter at the Burger King down the block. Large fries and jumbo soda for everyone and a strawberry shake for Val. Suzy gets her wedding gift in hard cash and off she goes to the races. An hour or so later Richard is up in the office (naysayers like me not having been invited to the dance) gushing over my desk, giving me the blow-by-blow of the whole glorious event.

His doomed spasm of joy is almost too sad to watch.

The next day Richard is back sporting a fresh round of sad laments. He slinks into a chair and lobs them at me one by one, while Valentine waddles breathlessly around the office, a world of wonder in her big black eyes, opening every drawer, picking up every phone, grabbing every sheet of paper, twisting every knob, oblivious of the turmoil into which she has been born. Richard's eyes keep track of her spree of abandon, but from some far distance.

"I can't believe it," he all but whines. "Suzi even charged me to go to bed with her on our honeymoon night."

For the New Year's issue of *Street News*, we dress Valentine up as the incoming year and put her picture on the cover. "A New Beginning," it says.

Richard buys twenty copies.

One Friday night I'm sitting at my computer, pretending to work. But my mind is not in it.

My mind is out the window.

My soul is in the pipe.

And just as I'm preparing to go out and give my demons another pound of flesh, the phone rings.

It's Richard.

He's calling from a Jersey jail.

The cops at Port Authority yanked him.

He had no ID.

They ran his name through the computer.

The warrant popped up.

Suzi is nowhere to be found.

And the nurse from Child Services watching Valentine is already two hours into overtime. There's no one else.

"Suzi's probably beamed up somewhere," Richard says. "Look, I know you're probably busy, but could you go over to my house and stay with Valentine until Suzi gets home? There's plenty of food in the fridge."

"Of course I'll do it," I tell him, the glory of being needed greater, for the moment, than my urge to fry my brains. But I pack my pipe and lighter out of dumb habit.

As I step out onto Ninth Avenue, I see the dealers are out.

They know me.

They sidle up.

They say, "Got it good."

But I'm on a different mission.

"Later," I tell them. "Later," and step around.

Down the block the girls are out. They suspect, by my purposeful stride, that I have just copped some goodies. I survey their expectant faces, but no sign of Suzi among them. For a second I resent her, off partying somewhere, carefree, while I'm about to be tied down with her child.

But not really.

I'm needed.

The nurse is packed up when I arrive.

Ready and waiting to go.

Valentine is standing near the living room window with her back to me, as if concealing her embarrassment. She has one hand up, resting on the seat of a chair to steady herself.

The nurse curtly points out the things I might need.

—Clean diapers over here.

—Bottle up there.

—Formula in the cabinet.

Then she is out the door.

At the sound of the door banging shut, Valentine turns herself around—unsteadily, but with amazing dignity—and peers past me to the closed door.

She blinks once...

Looks up at me...

Her lips begin to quiver...

And in the next second she is wailing away. It comes from deep in her gut and pours out of her little mouth, emptying her completely. She has to gasp for breath before each terrible howl.

I go down on one knee to comfort her.

But none of my dumb child-pleaser shtick has any effect.

Not goo-goo eyes.

Not hide-a-face.

Not even wiggly ears.

She just stands there consumed by her misery.

I phone my editor, Janet. She has just become a mother herself. She'll know what to do. We talk briefly, Valentine sobbing all the while. I can't hear much through the din, but enough to discover that Janet has no secrets to tell me. I am unsettled by this revelation—that all women are not born with maternal magic encoded in their genes. I hang up in total dismay.

I draw Valentine over to me on the couch.

I look her dead in the eyes.

I see tears have crusted on her cheek, clear as crystal, like crushed diamonds. But I find no clue in her face to the source of her pain. And then, I can't tell you why, maybe because of her name, but whatever the reason, I begin to softly sing.

My little Valentine…

My funny Valentine…

You always smile when skies are gray…

…And to my amazement this works. Valentine stops crying as abruptly as she had started and stares back at me with profound curiosity. I feel an odd, sudden flush of gratitude.

Your lips are laughable…

Unphotographable…

Stay, little Valentine, stay…

I keep on singing, afraid to stop, panicking over the words, humming when they don't come, and suddenly, four verses in, the whole thing strikes me as absurdly funny. I imagine my dealer standing in the doorway watching. Eight o'clock Friday night in the heart of Hell's Kitchen, people chasing demons all up and down the darkness outside, let's go see what Lee is up to.

I'm cracking myself up.

Head tilted back—

Eyes up at the ceiling—

Laughing right out loud—

And Valentine joins right in.

Flaps her little arms up and down like wings and howls with delight. Her joy like a fragile gift.

I feel higher than I have in years.

When Suzi strides through the door several hours later, I am amazed at how suddenly maternal she becomes. With deft efficiency she swoops up Valentine, gathers her into her night things, and hauls her off to bed. I sit watching her, a bystander now. With each assured twist and turn of her firm body, my empathy for Richard grows. I can almost taste her juiciness.

Richard gets something like thirty days in prison. And no sooner is he released than he is in my office, bemoaning yet another slight in life. His lawyer—the same one who negotiated his windfall settlement—has saddled him with a $20,000 tab for representing him on the warrant case—about $18,000 too much for the work.

"You have a way with words," says Richard flatteringly. "I wanna do a letter to this shyster on the computer."

Drawing on my vast store of legal knowledge, gleaned from watching numerous episodes of *L.A. Law*, I imply, in so many well-chosen words, that a malpractice suit is not only in order here but is definitely in the offing. Richard takes this to his lawyer, triumphantly returns, clutching a check for seven grand, and hits me off with a C-note.

Being in the can, it seems, was just the grist Richard needed for his muse. According to him, his rhymes went over in a big way on the inside, and his poet's cap now firmly back on his head, he has written an ode to Valentine. He stands over me like an expectant father as I read the thing—singsong rhyme, rap-song intonations. I don't recall the words. But it has Valentine out there already, a big, bad hot mama, taking the streets by storm.

On Valentine's birthday Richard shows up and invites me for coffee. We stop, on the way, to pick up ice cream, cake, and other party goodies.

"We're having a party for Valentine," he chirps. "Why don't you come over."

We haul the stuff up to his apartment, six flights up.

"You'll have to excuse Suzi," he says off-handedly. "She's not completely awake yet. She had a rough night."

Valentine and I play as Richard disappears past the kitchen to drag Suzi out of bed. She comes out in a tattered robe, puffy-eyed and short-tempered. When she speaks to Richard at all, she wields his name like a razor.

"Here we are!" says Richard, perky as a virgin coed, his insistent merriment beginning to grate even on my nerves. It reminds me of the one and only time my father invited me over to his house. He was so solicitous of my enjoyment, asking me again and again if I was having fun, that all I wanted to do was clamp my hands around his throat and squeeze.

It's just the four of us. We all gather around, Suzi prefacing every concession she makes to this with a tired sigh. We eat ice cream and cake, push smiling faces Valentine's way, sing "Happy Birthday" perfectly off-key, Valentine blinking back at us all the while, wondering at our odd behavior. I give it my best effort. But all I keep thinking, my eyes floating from Valentine to Richard to Suzi, is how very, very hard a lonely person will try.

I once wrote an ad for Richard. He imagined that he could wholesale his poems to *Street News* readers, and asked for my help. The ad read, "The street rhymes. It rhymes in the heart of the man who sings its song."

10

On **every** **smut** **film** crew there is a particular individual whose sole function is to make it hard for the leading man, so to speak, should his costar prove inadequate to the task.

This person is known as the "fluffer."

And I'm sitting on the set of the *Geraldo* show, me and three fellow *Street News* vendors, miked up and ready to roll, when this youngish, slicked-up brother, looking like he just slid off the cover of *GQ*, ambles over, crouches in front of us, and levels a 2,000-watt smile in our eyes.

"You see those two ladies over there?" he says in a perfectly modulated voice, pointing to the housewifey duo sitting a discreet distance stage left of us.

"They are the enemy." He frowns, "They hate the sight of homeless people and they don't care about your problems. All they want is to get people like you out of their neighborhood. So when we start rolling, don't be shy about letting them know exactly what you think of them."

At first I'm somewhat encouraged by this apparent empathy, even though I find the guy a little too operatic. Only, a minute later I spot him out of the corner of my eye, kneeling in front of the two ladies now, and pointing his manicured, muckraking finger in our direction.

So, I say to myself, *a fluffer.*

I suppose I wasn't thinking too clearly at the time. I mean I could say I wasn't actually excited about going on *Geraldo*, a show I hadn't once watched without wincing. But there's no denying that when his producer, Bill Lancaster, called *Street News*, trawling for real, live homeless people to participate in a segment concerning the notorious Larry Hogue, I jumped at the chance.

A little history is in order here:

In the seventies Geraldo Rivera was a local ABC News grunt of ambiguous ethnicity—having romanticized the Jerry Rivers moniker his mixed, Jewish-Hispanic parents had tagged him with—when he began to make a name for himself by turning in gripping, impassioned pieces that advocated for the little guy.

Such was the treatment he gave a story about Willowbrook, a state mental hospital where for years patients had been warehoused, amid deplorable conditions, with little if any attention paid to rehabilitation. Where a Mike Wallace type might have scored points by ambushing hospital administrators, cameras rolling, Geraldo leveled his passions at the plight of the patients, crying real, on-camera tears and creating such public outcry that the politicians jumped in demanding sweeping policy changes.

As a result, New York State mental hospitals were no longer

permitted to keep committed any patient who could be stabilized through self-administered medication. This brought on the wholesale release of thousands of borderline mentally ill. And Geraldo was hailed as something of a champion of the victimized, an image he enjoyed right up until his later falling out with ABC.

But problems with the newly liberated patients began to surface over the next decade, the foremost of which was a catch-22 situation whereby medications were so effective in normalizing patients that some stopped taking them regularly and would therefore lapse back into psychotic behavior. Another problem was that, though they were stabilized, a number of the outpatients still had difficulty managing their affairs on their own and wound up living on the street, many of them supported by monthly SSI disability checks.

This had been Larry Hogue's story. Not only did he regularly neglect to take his meds, he started medicating himself with crack instead. And when he was cracked up, he stalked the streets making a frightening spectacle of himself. He had a particular affinity for the Upper West Side. It's likely that at one time he found some degree of compassion among its liberal-minded denizens, but under the influence of his habit, he quickly wore out his welcome.

Officials proclaimed that their hands were tied. They could arrest him and take him to a psych ward for observation, but once he ceased to be an imminent threat to himself and others, they were powerless, under the new order of things, to keep him off the streets.

However, a front-page story in the *West Side Spirit*, which tagged Hogue as the Wild Man of Ninety-sixth Street and documented what a pariah he had become, roused public outrage—as had Geraldo's earlier story on Willowbrook, ironically—and, following a brief tug-of-war between the ACLU and police authorities, Larry was finally committed long-term. Janet Wickenhaver, editor of the *Spirit* and author of the piece, received a journalism award for her efforts.

But the fact remained that there existed no authority for permanently institutionalizing mental patients. And after barely a year of confinement, Larry Hogue was deemed, by whatever standards they measure such things, fit enough to leave the facility.

By now, Wickenhaver was plying the other side of the street, in a sense, as the new editor-in-chief of *Street News*, where, by a vigorous process of attrition, I had ascended to the rank of senior editor and clandestine nightly residence in the office.

As for Geraldo, he was long gone from his ABC post and was now mining the syndicated talk-show game for big bucks. And what his producers foresaw was that upon Larry Hogue's release, there was yet more grist to be milled from *his* sad odyssey.

The synergy of it all was mind-boggling.

So when Lancaster calls asking if I and some of the vendors would be interested in coming on the show, I say yes.

"Splendid!" he says. "What would be ideal is if I could come over there and preinterview your people. Do you think you could round up maybe half a dozen of them in your office by, say, six o'clock?"

I am already behind deadline with an editorial I had promised. Janet is downtown, huddled with the art director, putting the issue together, expecting my piece within the hour, and I am having one of those days when the English language seems like a foreign and perplexing curiosity.

But it is too late.

I have caught *Geraldo* fever.

"No problem," I assure Lancaster.

Of course Lancaster thinks this is "splendid," too, and he assures me there'll be a hundred dollars in it for me as the lead man, and a "travel allowance" for each vendor who appears on the show. I promptly feed this news down the pipeline to Barbara Bales at *Street News'* tiny storefront distribution office on West Forty-sixth Street, squeezed between a bodega without any visible customers and a five-story walkup. By five-thirty that evening I have half a dozen anxious candidates milling around the office, lured by the prospects of fifteen minutes' fame and a pair of crisp twenties as a kiss-off.

Only, Lancaster never shows.

And when I call his office, no one seems to know precisely where he is. This doesn't exactly endear me to my fellow vendors, who have each sacrificed the meat of their rush-hour trade on my word. Quelling their rising apprehension doesn't mix well with getting on with the writing I have to do.

By seven o'clock things are on the verge of getting ugly.

"If he's not here in fifteen minutes," I decide, "I'll see if I can get you each ten free papers for your trouble."

Just then the phone sings out.

I snatch it up.

It's Lancaster.

"My apologies," he says, his Aussie lilt tending toward a squeak. "But C. Vernon Mason backed out at the last minute. I've got to zip up to Harlem and try to bring him back to the fold."

That is a tension breaker. The thought of Lancaster wielding his golly-by-Jove perkiness above 110th Street gives me a genuine chuckle.

"But not to worry," he assures me. "We've already shelled out thirty-five hundred for studio time. We'll have some kind of Larry Hogue show, and you'll be involved. But at this point we're not sure what it will be. You'll just have to hang in."

This news doesn't go down too well with the vendors. I get on the phone to stump for the ten freebies. They'd have to come out of the office's supply.

"How's it going?" Janet wants to know as soon as she gets on the line.

"Great. I just heard back from Geraldo's people," I gush, knowing full well that isn't the thing she is asking about. "They're going ahead with the Hogue thing and definitely want some of our vendors involved. It should be great publicity for us."

"Good," she says.

"There's just one little hitch. I had these guys waiting up here and Lancaster couldn't show. I thought I'd give them ten free papers each."

"What about your copy?" she asks.

Janet cut her teeth as a reporter on the *Bergen Record*, a city daily in New Jersey. She is trying her best to impose a sense of journalistic urgency on the hodgepodge of hapless souls now laboring under the *Street News* masthead, the most delinquent of whom is yours truly.

We affectionately refer to her as the editrix.

"I'm hammering away," I lie.

"Well, hammer faster or I'll have to cut your piece."

"Sure thing," I sing. "What about the papers?"

"How many are planning to come to this party?"

"Well, I got six vendors up here."

"Okay. Six and no more. And I want a signature from each person who gets them."

"Will do."

She signs off with a parting warning: Tomorrow morning latest with my copy or it's out. I pull an all-nighter, fortified by several cups of house blend from Empire Coffee, two doors down, whose brew packs a wallop like a line of Bolivian Flake. One cup and I'm usually good for four pages of crisp copy. The piece comes together, around three in the morning, in one, manic, pulse-pounding gush—nothing like a little sleep deprivation to loosen one's narrative flow—and I have two thousand muscular words on the "politics of assumption." I fax it downtown right then and there.

Let Janet see that *when she comes in in the morning*, I tell myself, and feeling like a master at the top of his form, I crash on the couch in the back of the office.

Janet calls at 9:15 A.M. sharp.

"I got your piece," she says.

I wasn't expecting any raves from her. She tended to play it close to the chest with me. She suspected that I had a poor, tired huddling mass of ego, yearning to be free, and she wasn't about to offer it refuge on the pages of *Street News*.

"So whaddya think?" I ask, poised to pick up on any congratulatory nuance her voice might betray.

"I got two paragraphs into it," she says, "before I lost my will to live."

Definitely not a rave.

In the heat of writing the piece I thought I had been keenly insightful. But it wouldn't be the first time yesterday's gem turned into mere paste on a second, sober reading.

"I'm sorry," she says, "but I have to go with another piece."

I am burning, but I don't give her any argument. The place to have made my point was on the page.

Twenty minutes later Lancaster is on the phone.

"Mason's out," he announces, trying his best to sound as if it

138

was his decision. "But we're going ahead. You still have your people?"

"I can round them up again," I tell him, not at all sure that I can.

That's splendid, too, he tells me.

They will be expecting us at two o'clock.

There'll be lunch waiting in the green room.

Lunch waiting in the green room, I repeat to myself.

But what I am thinking is, here is my chance to redeem my just-battered self-esteem. Determined that by two o'clock I be the supremely informed homeless sage of daytime TV, I pull out our clip files and dive into them.

Geraldo fever has me completely inflamed.

In person the *Geraldo* set looks genuinely cheesy—little more than a few bland cardboard flats and ratty plastic potted plants. And of course everything is smaller and more cramped than it appears on the TV screen.

The *Street News* contingent is now down to four. Besides myself there's Wayne Elliot, soft-spoken and freckle-faced, who plies papers in the theater district and manages to keep an SRO roof over his head from the proceeds; Harvel Ford, a Vietnam vet now on the verge of getting his culinary-arts certificate so that he can pursue his dream of being a chef; and finally there's Carl Scheabel, the wild card of the bunch. He has made no concession to his TV debut and is garbed in the same ratty clothes he had on when I last saw him. He has often boasted of having particular cunning by virtue of his mixed Sicilian-

German-Jewish ancestry. I tease him that he should have been shot at birth.

But what Carl is most is a pathological liar. And the more outrageous the lie, the more calmly and convincingly he puts it forth. I am expecting trouble from his lips.

In the green room we are given a quick pep talk on the dos and don'ts of video glory: Don't put your hand in your face when you're speaking. Be careful not to touch the pin-on mike. Talk to Geraldo, not to the camera. A guy drifts in with a bunch of numbered file cards and tells us each to put our name and affiliation on them. Then the stage manager appears and ushers us into the studio and onto the set where we are joined by two other homeless guys, both acquaintances of Larry Hogue. I assume this overkill on street types is in compensation for the fact that Larry himself is not there.

A few minutes later the stage manager yells, "Stand by," the Quiet sign blinks on, and suddenly the room is bathed in hot white light. A bit of theme music is pumped through the studio speakers, the announcer chirps an introduction, and with a burst of applause Geraldo descends the center aisle of the studio bleachers like a prizefighter entering the arena, an image helped along by his battered nose (the legacy of a chair-throwing melee during a previous broadcast featuring a contingent of neo-Nazis).

"Larry Hogue," he declares curtly. "The Wild Man of Ninety-sixth Street. I want you all to take a look at this."

The lights dim slightly.

The studio monitors flare up.

There on the screen we see clandestine footage of Hogue, dancing in and out of traffic, lurching at startled passersby, leering at terrified old ladies, brandishing a piece of wood from a construction site, and otherwise damning himself and all like him. When the lights come back up, all you can hear is the low whir of the air-conditioning.

"I want you to meet someone," Geraldo says into his close-up camera as he approaches the two ladies sitting on the set. He introduces them—one from Long Beach, California, and the other from Manhattan's Upper West Side—giving them the Howard Beale treatment, declaring, in so many words, that they are mad as hell and not going to take it anymore.

"You are from the neighborhood where Larry Hogue had his reign of terror," he tells Ms. Upper West Side. "Tell me, what do you want to tell these homeless people sitting here?"

One of the cameras has swung over to her and now its red light pops on. The monitor screen is filled by her worried face as Geraldo, the studio audience, and millions of viewers await her reply. But before she speaks, she makes one tactical mistake. She takes a quick gander to her right. And what she sees, gazing back at her, ready to pounce on her every utterance, is what looks like a small army of precisely the same people who had scared her whole neighborhood shitless.

"Well," she says somewhat hoarsely, blinking in our direction, her knitted fingers a writhing, pink pet in her lap. "There are a lot of unfortunate people on the streets," she declares.

"They don't have it easy," she mulls.

"They need special care and services," she concludes.

"And they're not really getting it," she summarizes.

"They need to be provided for."

Ms. Long Beach who is sitting next to her during all this, imitates a dashboard ornament as her head bobs earnest agreement with every syllable out of her mad-as-hell compatriot's Upper West Side mouth.

Instead of the much-hyped showdown between the unwanted-of-the-streets and a populace that has grown hostile toward them, what Geraldo now has is eight people sitting on stage, all of whom stand ready to plead righteous compassion for the plight of the homeless. And try as he might, going back and forth—coast to coast as it were—between Long Beach and the West Side of Manhattan, he cannot provoke anything more from them than unbridled concern for the welfare of the less fortunate. Out there in TV land, rumble-hungry Geraldo fans are already consulting their *TV Guides* and reaching for their remotes. I peer around for any sight of the fluffer, but he is nowhere to be found.

"We have some people here from *Street News*, the homeless paper," Geraldo announces, resorting to the prepared file cards.

The camera pans across our faces as he introduces us one by one. When he gets to Carl's card, he has to look at it twice.

"It says here, Mr. Scheabel," Geraldo notes, eyes lifting from the card with the greatest reluctance, "that you are a doctor of physics."

"Yup, that's right," sings Carl in his boardroom baritone, "Ph.D."

I can hear Harvel snickering next to me.

He bangs me on the thigh with the back of his hand.

All I can do is stare at the floor.

"You must have a hard life," Geraldo mutters skeptically. "May I ask where you received your degree?"

"University of Heidelberg, Baden-Baden, Germany, 1974." Carl shoots back, batting nary an eyelash.

"Mr. Scheabel," Geraldo says, testily dropping the *Carl* "You knew you were going to be on the show today. Didn't it occur to you to change your clothes? Put on a fresh shirt?"

"This is a fresh shirt," Carl says.

With that the audience begins to snicker, and Harvel all but tumbles out of his chair. Geraldo stands there glaring at Carl. The hand with the cards drops to his side.

"We'll be back," he says softly.

The theme music pipes up, the camera sweeps across the audience, the applause swells quickly to a peak, then dies a quick death, the red lights go out on the cameras, the studio lights go dim, technicians flutter in, and Geraldo disappears into the wings. Two minutes later the whole process reverses itself and we are back on the air. Geraldo stands in the middle of the bleachers, curtly announces that the topic of the show is not about the homeless but about "people at risk," and puts his back to us, thereby signifying that he has had quite enough input from homeless people for one day, thank-you-very-much.

Off he plunges into the audience, challenging every pat assumption, amplifying every timid point, trawling for any semblance of a debatable issue. It's a game effort, there's a trickle of sound and fury here and there, but it's coming mostly from him. Prone to herd instinct, the audience has already taken its cue from the Samaritan tone with which the show began.

Meanwhile we're sitting on the set like so much useless baggage, packed, but no place to go, me thumbing through a handful of crib notes, poised to put fact and figure behind my every sterling observation. Each time Geraldo turns toward the set, I try my best to look bright and eager. But he never calls on me. I made my own tactical error, I later surmised. A day before the show I faxed Geraldo's office a copy of an editorial I had written about Jeffrey Rose, another at-large mental patient, who had stabbed a child with a pen. The neighborhood block association where he did this had worked itself into an angry, moblike froth over the incident, and I made the thrust of my piece an appeal to reason. That was okay for a *Street News* editorial, but reason doesn't play too well on TV. I had inadvertently maneuvered myself out of the loop.

As we wing our way to the show's dismal end, Geraldo comes

up with a clinical psychiatrist, seated in the front row, who has made a specialty of addressing "people at risk."

"Tell me, Doctor," Geraldo wants to know once he has established the man's bona fides, "what is the psychiatric community's position on the subject of people at risk?"

The doctor clears his throat, and in slightly smug but refreshingly psychobabble-free language, says that over the last decade he and his colleagues have observed an increase in the number of mentally disturbed people wandering the streets who are not getting the medical care and attention they require, and for whom he feels society has an obligation to provide. In the dead silence in which this jewel of profundity is received, I can swear I hear Geraldo's teeth grinding.

The show goes downhill from there. Geraldo ignores his treacherous panel altogether, doesn't dare resort to his file cards, glares now and then at his two turncoat "irate" ladies—who look as if they can't wait to bolt from their seats and flee to the sanctuary of their living room couches, from which perspective *Geraldo* looks a lot more viewer-friendly.

When it is all over, the lights go out, the audience is let out through a side door, a production assistant pushes money-thick envelopes into our hands and quickly hustles us out of the building as if we all have communicable diseases.

I devote my money to enough recreational self-destruction to put the whole experience—and subsequent thoughts on the futility of being a party to the mass-media mill—firmly out of my mind. When the show actually airs, I don't even bother watching it.

11

I was having a real bad Tuesday.

First the subway, and now this. The transit undercovers had been out in full force on the train and it had taken me all morning and most of the afternoon playing hide-and-seek with them to scare up twenty-two bucks selling *Street News*.

All I wanted after that was a little diversion from my frustration.

There is a spot uptown only two blocks from the subway exit and—patience never being the virtue of a man out to get himself a good buzz—they usually get my money.

But no one is there.

I walk to the corner, down the block to the projects, stroll through the courtyard, eyes left and right, but they are nowhere to be found. I come back up to Lexington, walk uptown five blocks, turn, and stroll up toward Madison. There are plenty of people on the street, but none with that hooded, inquisitive look in their eyes that asks those who know, *How many?*

"I hate this shit," someone says over my shoulder just as I'm about to make another round of the whole mess.

—Another one looking:

Tall, dark, and ragged, cop money scrunched in his fist.

"Man, I hate it when they all close down at the same time," he grumbles.

Of course he knows I'm looking too.

It's a kind of radar we have.

"You try the projects yet?" he wants to know.

I give him a slow-disgusted-*yes*, shake of the head.

"Dead," I tell him.

But hope springs eternal, even in a crackhead's heart.

He peels off in that direction anyway.

I go all the way down to First Avenue, to the other projects over there. Sometimes they come out with three-dollar jammies. The quality is sporadic, but I'm in no position to be picky. I want a hit and I want it now.

When I get there, a few kids are hanging out along the wall by the Qwik Stop Deli. They know what's up. They know what I'm there for. They eye me with bemused derision. Another druggie sniffing around their hood.

But there's nothing happening.

Back I go to where I started.

I'm standing by the subway, craning my neck to see down the block, trying to make out who among the few stragglers there might be pitching, when I spot Tall, Dark, and Ragged heading back my way. I can tell—by the bulge of his eyes and the tick in his neck—

that he's found a live spot.

"Projects," he blurts as he swoops by me without pause, skeed to the max, eyes scanning left and right like twin satellite dishes.

"You best hurry up," he adds, throwing the words over his shoulder as he disappears down the block.

Shit, you don't have to tell me twice.

I as good as run, eating up sidewalk in long, rapid strides. And as I hit the avenue, I fall in step with a salt-and-pepper duo—one a dread-headed Rasta, the other a hippie-haired blonde—and it looks like we're all headed for the same place.

Only, something's not right about them.

Their jeans are just a bit too clean.

Their sneakers are too fresh.

And both have obviously made good use of their razors and combs.

Undercovers, I'm thinking. *Maybe that's why everything has gone dead. The cops must be doing one of their buy-and-bust sweeps.*

I throttle back a little, let them keep a few paces on me.

Two street types zip by me as I reach the projects, hurrying up the block, fists buried in their pockets. I can tell they've just copped something.

They have my envy.

We all love smoking. But nobody likes copping.

Inside the courtyard a steerer is perched on a stump-jumper

bike—the kind with its main frame mounted on twin heavy-gauge springs that eat up bumps and curbs. He does his job—pointing Salt and Pepper to the far fence, where the pitcher stands serving up dimes from a small brown bag—and the two of them saunter over there.

That's the thing.

They saunter.

Too casual to be honest pipeheads.

Got to be cops, I tell myself, and still, being so close, it's all I can do to hang back a minute, put my back to the pitcher, and take a casual bystander pose, ready to stroll off at any sudden sound of a scuffle.

They don't have any reason to come after me, I tell myself. *I'm clean. It's the dealer they want, anyway.*

Then I hear PAP! PAP! PAP! PAP! PAP!

It's funny how the sound of real gunfire is dry and empty. Not at all like in the movies. But you recognize the sound immediately, even if you've never heard it before. When I turn around, Salt and Pepper are gone and the dealer is down—dead before he hit the ground.

Five shots to the head at close range.

Whoever it was who wanted him dead really wanted him.

"Shit!" the steerer says, slams his butt down on the bike, and jets across the courtyard in a frenzy of pumping knees. But I just stand there, rooted.

This has happened to me before. Late one night several years ago in midtown. A young Asian had been thoroughly gut-stabbed by a bouncer outside a rough-trade joint on Eighth Avenue and had staggered away to the gutter and collapsed. I rushed over, hoping somehow it would come to me what to do when I got to him. But it was already all over. I reached him just in time to see the last breath sigh out of his body. The same strange, frightening fascination at seeing death up close and for real that I had felt then, is what has me momentarily riveted now.

I hear a sudden terrified shriek cut across the courtyard and bounce off the project walls. A young woman comes careening from the building behind the fence crying out the dead man's name. She crumbles to her knees when she reaches him, drops herself over his prone body, buries her face in his blood and bone, and wails away, making opera of her shock and grief.

A few seconds later a pair of Housing cops walk out the door. They seem so bored and matter-of-fact, loping along, you'd think they were on their way to lunch.

No need to rush.

Just another dead nigger.

All in a day's work.

They survey the scene with shocking nonchalance, cursory glances this way and that, as if the shooters might be leaning on the fence waiting to be cuffed, smoking guns in their hands. Neither of them seems interested in asking anyone what happened or who saw what. Nor does it occur to me that I could give them a pretty good description. All that's going through my mind is acid and vitriol for bad timing and rotten luck.

If only I had gotten here a few minutes sooner to cop.

That's the kind of bad Tuesday I'm having.

I'm out of there on a slow stroll, bitching and moaning all the way. *Now there'll be cops crawling all over the place,* I grouse to myself. *I'll never get anything now.* It's a particular dread that overtakes you when you're a seasoned pipehead, all primed for a hit, and can't get so much as a crumb; a slow sinking panic that starts low in your gut, then eats its way to the center of your brain.

I hit the first bodega I come to for a cut-rate forty-ounce malt liquor and wander around for the next half hour sucking it down, trying to douse the rising fire, and hoping beyond hope that some enterprising wannabe will take advantage of the distraction and put out a quick bundle or two of product on his competitor's turf. It's happened before. They even have a name for it. They call it scraping customers.

But mostly they're like steam, these pitchers.

When things heat up they're vapor.

I've got plenty of company now: other pipeheads looking piqued and ill-tempered, hovering around the dead crack spots, wondering why—when they got all day to blow a nigger away—this shit has to happen now.

Just then I think I can see them coming out of a tenement.

Two that look the type:

Low-worn oversize trousers.

Designer logos screaming from their jackets.

Neck and fingers sporting gold.

Ditty-bop, one-leg-pumping, head-tilted-to-the-side step.

"'Sup?" says the one on the right with a backward jut of his head.

I walk over to him. Just a kid really, but already hard as nails.

"Choo need?"

"Dimes?" I ask with weak hope.

"How many," he says.

"Gimme two," I say, all sunshine and roses now.

We do it on the down-low, brushing by each other, making the switch-off with fast fingers. I press the money into his hand, he drops the little baggies in my palm. Off I scramble in a fever, stem already in my hand, tearing the bag open with my teeth, squeezing the stuff out into my palm, thumbing it into the pipe—all the while looking left, right, ahead, behind, for any prying eyes. But then, from biting the bag open, a bitter, all-too-familiar sliminess hits the tip of my tongue and the whole world spins out from under me.

Stupid, thirsty, dumb-ass fuck!

Twenty dollars for two pieces of soap.

The thirsties will get you every time.

No doubt about it. I was having a real bad Tuesday.

Now I'm stalking toward downtown in a white heat, eighty

153

cents left in my pocket, every nerve in my body screaming for a hit, no place to dump my rage and even less room for my dread. The rush hour has come and gone. And as the dinner hour plays out and the sun slowly dies, the streets begin to buzz with night people strolling from the restaurants, wandering in and out of stores, walking their dogs, stalking in and out of bars, queuing up for movies, running for the buses, waving for taxicabs.

It's all money on the hoof.

And me with eighty cents.

I see a guy come staggering down the sidewalk, turning down the side street now, so drunk he can barely stay erect. I tag along behind him. He blunders his way into a four-story building. When I peer, in I see him in the vestibule, leaning against the wall and digging for his keys. But he's really blitzed. He can't even find his pockets. And I say to myself, *Lord, don't let me do what I'm thinking*, because I may be a pipehead, I'll give you that, but this "what I'm thinking" isn't me.

Just then he looks up, notices me standing outside, and blinks dumbly out at me, too drunk or too stupid to be scared, even though I'm not out to do anything to him.

I swear to God I'm not.

Not a fucking thing.

But I tell you I can *smell* the money in his pockets.

Money he'll never miss the morning after.

And there is no one else around.

"You need a hand?" I hear myself say.

And he says nothing. Just stands there hunched against the wall as I step inside, his face blank and curious as a two-year-old.

"Can I help you with your keys?"

I plunge my hand right down in his pocket, still thinking—praying even—*Lord, don't let me do it!* And my fingers find a wad as thick as a slab of meat. Enough to keep me buzzed for days.

But the Lord is answering prayers tonight.

Thirsty as I am, I just can't go there.

One look at the guy's face up close and all I can see is the sodden, vague misery there. He is having his own bad Tuesday, the sorry fuck.

I pull out his keys.

Open the door for him.

Hand him back the keys.

"There you go, buddy," I say with a piece of a smile in place.

"You'd better go up and sleep it off."

He gives me a jerky nod of his head in salute, gathers himself up, and hauls a buck from deep in his pocket, hands it to me, and disappears into the elevator.

I'm sweaty and trembling when I walk outside. I get only a few paces down the block before the consolation of having rendered a minor service begins to lose its blush and I'm pissed off at my own timidity.

But a buck will get me a beer, I tell myself.

I open the hand holding the bill, and the world spins upright again.

I'm staring a fifty dead in the face.

This time everyone is out uptown and anxious to make up for dollars lost. I have to all but beat them back with a stick. I cop my shit, dart around the nearest corner, and fill my lungs with the sweet caramel-and-ammonia-tasting smoke. My brain immediately leaps into hyperdrive. The streets suddenly crackle with electricity. Every slam of a car door, every fragment of far-off conversation, every distant screech of a tire, rushes, clear as crystal, to my ears. I want to do everything at once, but can decide on no one thing to do at all. Everything is a distraction. Down the streets I scramble, pulsing with eager anticipation. *Wherever the night takes me!* I tell myself.

But then the dry crack of a .38 and the echo of a woman shrieking replays itself in my ears. I am seized by a grim notion: *What if there's a bullet out there for me, ready to slam into the back of my skull any minute?* That, and the thought that I would deserve such a thing for what I had almost done—for what I will surely sooner or later do—overcomes all other rational thought. And treading back downtown, every nuance of the night now a fresh-born fear, the back of my neck tingling with bald, unrelenting, apprehension, my eyes going left and right like twin satellites, I pass a bank with a clock on the wall.

11:09 P.M. the digits read.

My Bad Tuesday still has fifty-one minutes to go.

12

I was smoked out, tapped out, thirsty as hell for another blast, dragging my ass in for the night with great reluctance, when, a few doors down the block, a woman's voice calls out to me. I can't see her face—she's standing, head stuck in the phone booth, receiver to her ear—but what I can see of her is in perfect proportion and tantalizingly blond on top.

Her hand shoots out, a cigarette daintily poised between her fingers, and she's jiggling the thing to let me know she needs a light. I walk over to her, fumbling in my pockets long enough to take a good gander, and she's almost breathtakingly good-looking; all creamy, homogenized lushness and beguiling emerald eyes—a glimmering spectacle against the drab, shuttered storefronts along Ninth Avenue.

I light her up and she yanks a drag from the thing before she turns and starts purring into the phone again, working away at a wad of gum all the while as if she doesn't have a care in the world, standing here in Hell's Kitchen at two-thirty in the morning, crack dealers to the left, junkies to the right, sodden barhoppers slouching along everywhere else.

I like that.

I'm a sucker for spunk.

All the same, in the face of her freshness and perkiness, I feel too wretched, slovenly, and shy of resources to hope to take this anywhere. I'm about to step off, in fact, when she arrests me with a single, skyward "wait a second" stretch of her forefinger.

So I stand there like a trained mutt while she goes on gabbing into the phone. But she's facing me now, giving me the slow once-over, sizing me up; a cool, studied, confident appraisal. I can't quite make out what she's saying, but I can hear her working that gum: moist, chewy sounds insinuating in my ears.

Finally I hear her say, "Okay," and she plunks the receiver down and steps over to me.

"Where ya headed?" she asks.

"Upstairs," I tell her, pointing to the *Street News* office a few doors down. She yanks another drag off the cigarette, releasing a cloud of smoke that draws my envy. "Can I impose on you for one of your cigarettes?" I add.

"It's no imposition," she tells me, and digs around in her tiny black purse. A wisp of fragrance tickles my nose as she takes her time lighting me up. She uses a pink Bic, which, I realize, she had all along.

"Who's up there?" she wants to know.

"Just me and a few thousand copies of *Street News*," I tell her, figuring a little charm won't hurt the situation.

"*Street News*," she says. "I've heard of that." She peers up at the windows with a frown. "Is it clean?"

I mull this one over.

On the one hand, sloppiness has become something of a life skill with me. On the other, the lady is on the verge of inviting herself up. I decide *clean* is a relative term.

"Sure," I tell her. "I mean you couldn't accuse me of being a neat-freak, but it's not unhygienic or anything."

"Can I smoke up there?" she asks, flashing a brand-new stem.

I had long ago arrived at the convenient conclusion that so long as I didn't bring it into the office, I had my drugging under control. But here was the kind of scenario I have imagined on countless penniless late nights spent jonesing for hit: A beautiful stranger looms out of the darkness, shows me a kilo of the good stuff, and says, "Anywhere we can get high?"

It's all I can do to keep from tripping over my feet as I usher her up the two flights of narrow stairs and into the office.

She takes in the whole loft—desks, chairs, computers, posters on the wall—before settling into an easy chair up front and breaking out the goodies.

"Give me your hand," she says, a small rock of crack on the tip of her forefinger. Holding my outstretched hand palm up in hers like a fortune teller, she presses the rock into it, sliding her forefinger down the heel of my hand to wipe off the crumbs.

It's a seductive bit of business.

But before she releases my hand, she tells me she's a working girl, she only goes with men for money, and right now she's on her break.

"Besides," she adds for good measure, "I don't really like men. I'm really into women." I don't buy this last bit. But it isn't something I care to debate at the moment. Alluring as she is, my eyes are on that rock.

"So tell me your name already," I say, a thousand different hopes galloping forth.

"Emerald," she chirps with a smile.

With that we both light up and take off for hyperspace.

Pretty soon Emerald is sounding my buzzer two or three nights out of the week, coming up between tricks for a sit-down and a blast. Somewhat overwhelmed by her, I never make a play for her. And this, I suppose, is the draw, that she has a safe haven in which to buzz her brains. She also seems to be genuinely interested in my work, even taking time to sit and read my latest stuff before firing up her pipe. I, of course, find this absolutely beguiling. I'm interested in her as well, but amid the business of getting and keeping a buzz, I only manage to coax out a few details from her. I find out she's from Canada originally, and that her father is long since dead, murdered when she was just a child, she claims, as a consequence of being mixed up with the mob. But how or when she came over to the States or at what point she started walking the street is not exactly clear, though seeing that she lacks the hardened look of a veteran

160

hustler, I assume that the hooking is a recent development, brought on by a hungry stem.

She's a quick study, though, and no slouch at playing the male of the species. One night I buzz her in and she comes stomping up the stairs in heels, wearing a long, stunning turquoise dress slit up the side to mid thigh, and so tight about the pelvis you can count the hairs down there. No sooner have I gazed upon this apparition than I see a young, slim, long-haired mope trailing meekly behind her like a puppy dog.

"This motherfucker keeps telling me he wants to eat my pussy," Emerald huffs, glaring at the boy as if her virtue were above all compromise. The boy peers at me with *May I?* wrinkling his pathetic face. Frankly, with Emerald looking like that, I'm having a hard time seeing the downside to his proposition. I keep my trap shut, though. This is Emerald's play. I'm just a thirsty bystander. After a second or so of silence, Emerald standing, arms crossed, chest heaving, in the center of the room, the mope meekly edges over to her and tries whispering something to her.

"I know, I know," she hollers, moving away from him, one hand balled into a fist. "If I let you eat my pussy, you'll give me money." Every time she spits out the words *eat* and *pussy*, puppy dog all but comes in his pants. Emerald is fully aware of this, I realize; and the more disgusted she pretends to be, the more excited lover boy gets.

"Lee," she says, fists on her hips, leaning back on one elegantly shod heel, "are you going to throw this faggot out of here, or what?

He wouldn't know what to do with a pussy if he got a hold of one."

Faced with this exquisite torture, the sap goes red. Being bodily thrown out by a six-foot-three black guy—even one wearing coke-bottle glasses—will be a pulse-pounding denouement to his dominatrix fantasy. But it would also make me a participant in the trick, and I'm not quite ready for that.

"Yo," I say with a palms-forward shrug, "if the lady don't want you up here, you gotta go."

"Fucker," Emerald mutters at him, and glides down into a chair.

It takes a second prod—only slightly more forceful this time—but he finally slinks out of the room, chin dragging all the way. Emerald bolts from the chair as soon as the door shuts behind him and runs to the window to make sure he has left the building. I peer over her shoulder in time to see him glumly moping down Ninth, pausing, every few steps, to glance back at the building. Satisfied, Emerald plunks back down in the chair, a Cheshire grin exploding on her face, and opens her closed fist. Two crinkled fifties and four fat red bags of crack lay in her palm.

"So," she says with a shit-eating grin, "you write anything new since I been here?"

You got to love the lady.

As summer comes on and the weather turns, the quality-of-life police get busy beating back enough midtown urban reality to reassure the careless and curious. Conspicuous consumption being the life-blood of New York City, it's even open season in Hell's Kitchen. So, as the mercury climbs, nights along Ninth Avenue become increasingly populous with ripe, festive game. And for a while it is Emerald and me against the world. She divesting pent-up suckers of their cash for a brief dalliance, and me ever ready for whatever odd surprise she brings through the door, helping her to send it all gloriously up in smoke.

One evening she shows up with a dark brother built like a prize-fighter and sporting shoulder-length dreadlocks. I can tell right off he's not one of her tricks.

"This is Blue," she announces. "My new man."

Blue nods *hi*, gives my hand a firm shake, looks around the room. Like Emerald, he's heard of *Street News*. He even cites something from a recent edition. But I don't immediately get why Emerald would need a pimp. So far she's been a regular cash machine on her own.

"Blue's gonna wait up here for me while I go out and work," she tells me, "if it's all right with you."

"No problem," I say, and Blue settles into a chair, then buries his nose in the *Daily News*. The O. J. Simpson trial has just begun and the papers are littered with accounts of it. And when I turn on my little black-and-white TV, there O.J. is again, that same dark, bug-eyed picture of him the press has used since the whole thing began. You'd think no other photo existed. Seeing, live-action, the same story he's been plodding through in the *News*, Blue sets his paper down and we both sit gaping at the screen for a while.

But I can't leave the silence alone.

"So, do you think he's guilty or innocent?" I ask him.

"Innocent," he says. Or at least he thought so until he saw a computer simulation on TV that showed just how O.J. could have done it.

"Did you see it?" he wants to know.

I haven't. I've simply refused to get swept up by O.J. mania.

"No," I tell him. "I must've missed it."

With this, Blue pulls himself out of the chair and, hulking over me—I'm sitting on a low chair—he pantomimes the whole grisly business, step by step, his comb standing in for the knife. He does it so adroitly, and with such conviction, it's frightening. When he sneaks up behind Nicole, locks her in a half nelson, and wrenches her head off with the knife, I can almost see the blood erupting from her jugular.

I don't mind the silence so much after that.

I keep my eyes glued to the TV and hope Emerald doesn't take too long. *If he makes any sudden moves,* I tell myself, *I can throw my chair through the window.*

Fortunately Emerald scores in little time, and before you know it, she and I are puffing away on our stems while Blue sits staring into the TV screen. Blue isn't interested in crack. While crack was becoming a rage on the streets, he was cooling his heels upstate, doing thirteen years the hard way for armed robbery. Now here he is, fresh out of the joint by weeks, and odd man out at our pipe party.

Emerald and Blue immediately become an "item," as they say. They even set up house in a rented room just across the Jersey line. On the nights they're in town, Emerald deposits Blue with me before she goes on the stroll. I'm not immediately thrilled with this arrangement. Prison hasn't exactly left Blue a happy camper, and his mirthless, stoic presence tends to cast a pall over my nightly devotion to bug-eyed bacchanal. Besides which, I soon discover he's the type of guy who takes your every utterance with the greatest of seriousness. Opine too cavalierly in his company, or come off a bit shaky on your facts, and he's right on your case.

To make a minor point one evening, while the two of us are sitting around killing time, I happen to toss off a remark about the original Jews being almost as black as me. No sooner do I get this out of my mouth than I see Blue's brow bunching up.

"Say that again?" he says. "What do you mean when you say *Jews*?"

Recognizing my mistake, I rephrase my statement to indicate that I am referring to the original Semites. But Blue is eager to expound.

"Well," he says, pulling half of the air in the room into his lungs, "you know, words have a tendency to mislead people. We're dealing with a certain geographical location and the cultures and religions of that area. So when we say the Jew, mind you, that among the Jewish people in that geographical location, pigmentation of the skin might have ranged some sixteen different shades. Descendants of African people, or Ethiopian people, or more precisely Egyptians, or Nubian people of their continent, on the first and second cataract, which was called the Nile Valley, which today we know as Egypt..."

My eyes glaze over.

It's an impressive rush of factoids—he easily knows more on the subject than I do, though that alone is no great feat—and he obviously takes great pride in imparting it. But in the way he works up to his point, taking the long way around, I get there way before he does. And when he finally wraps it up, all I want to do is put a cap on the whole niggling bother.

"So we're essentially saying the same thing," I say with finality. "That, generally speaking, the original Semites were a dark-skinned people."

But off he goes again, into endless, elliptical overkill, and another twenty minutes of my life wander by before he comes up for air. It's like listening to my old friend Bob once he's knocked back a good couple dozen beers.

I make a mental note to myself.

Don't say shit to Blue.

Over time, however, I warm a bit to Blue, and he a bit to me. This is not to say that we are ever buddy-buddy. The circumstances of our acquaintance haven't provided any opportunities for me to be the kind of stand-up guy that he has come to recognize as worthy of his full trust and loyalty. And for my part, I have always been uneasy with people and situations to which I can't quite find the key. But after months of being thrown together with him—at the end of Emerald's coattails—I can see that there is more to Blue than his ex-con resume would suggest. I can only imagine what an awesome, dogged task it must have been for him to have gotten through all the dry, daunting historical tomes that—it becomes increasingly evident—he has taken it upon himself to consume. For though Blue is not stupid by any means, he is not a quick study either. And the image I get of him sitting hours on end in the prison library is of a man who is driven to discover things about himself.

I know another ex-con or two. Short-timers mostly. And while prison has left them more lost than ever—bitter, angry, defeated—Blue seems to have settled something during the time he was locked behind bars and seems to have emerged with something more to hold onto than the bebop, gangsta hipsterism that passes for identity on the streets. Toward me he is always respectful, always asks to use the phone, the john, the TV—which is something I can't say of Emerald—and big as he is, he never pushes his weight. I haven't a clue as to his ambitions—and perhaps neither does he—but I'd be hard pressed to doubt his ability to get there whenever he decides where he wants to go.

The only force that might throw him off his game is his obsession with Emerald. What a mouthwatering morsel she must have been to Blue, fresh from thirteen years in captivity, living cheek-by-jowl with hardened men. I can see why he dogged her steps until she finally agreed to go out with him. And I can see how genuinely gratified he is at having won her as a prize. But I can also see—having spent the last decade at the end of a crack pipe—that like me, Emerald would have to go down for a count before it would ever again be about love. Crack is a whole universe, not just a drug. And it needs to be filled with usable things. And in Emerald's line of work, having as big, strong, and streetwise a man as Blue on your wing can be very useful indeed.

As winter begins to bear down on the city, TNT—the Tactical Narcotics Team—begins to bear down as well, scooping up third-tier crack pitchers by the vanful all up and down Ninth Avenue. To maintain our spirits one particularly dry night, Emerald and I are sitting around the office drowning ourselves in beer. In contrast it's such a gentle wave, this crackless high, and we lean back into it so effortlessly that something passing for intimacy seems to pervade the moment. Emerald is so much softer on beer than she is on crack, sitting doe-eyed and demure in the easy chair, feet tucked under her, quietly reading one of my articles, that it is all I can do not to blurt out some kind of declaration to her about something.

"A little like the old days," I say.

"Yeah. We had fun, didn't we?" she replies, her green eyes climbing up to mine. "Blue's a pain in the ass, isn't he?"

"That's not what I meant," I tell her, wondering what it was I did mean, going white under the wattage of her gaze.

Blue is holding her back, she says. Though where she'd otherwise be headed she doesn't say.

"I've got to get rid of him, man," she says. "I just can't take it when he's around. He fucks up my high."

I would once have agreed with her, but not anymore. As cumbersome as he is in debate, Blue is a hell of a storyteller. When he starts spinning tales culled from his brilliant career knocking over jewelry stores, he is vivid and cinematic, serving up the close-ups, quick cuts, and snippets of dialogue with an aplomb that would make Spielberg sick with envy. Perhaps this is what irks Emerald: Sometimes she has to yield the spotlight to Blue.

"We don't have sex, you know," she blurts, now stretching her body, giving me the benefit of a full view. "I mean, not in the normal way."

"No?" I say despite myself, it really not being something I should hear.

"He's got this problem with the tip of his thing," she says. "It's too sensitive. It hurts too much for him to have sex. At least not with his thing."

This revelation makes Blue seem less intimidating somehow—there's nothing so human as a bit of frailty. But it's such an intimate detail that even though I am aware Emerald is opening the door for me, playing the Unfulfilled Woman, I feel something like a Peeping Tom. And that causes just enough hesitation and then I am on to her: It's not my body she's after but to keep alive my hunger for hers.

It's part of her catalog of useful things.

It is all too obvious now that Blue is no pimp. Not really. A pimp deals with women out of a certain contempt. But Blue just worships the ground Emerald walks on and takes her any way she comes. So far he has been little more than a handy utensil, kept on the shelf just in case. I wait for the day when he will get fed up with the constant idleness and erupt, but it never comes. In fact he seems to grow more docile by the day. I wonder what deep charms Emerald wields to keep him that way until I begin to discover empty glassine bags in the bathroom trash. I know dope isn't Emerald's thing. If she's doing it at all, it's because she finds it useful, to help take the edge off her crack high, for instance.

...And to help take the edge off of Blue.

It starts with him sniffing a dime bag a day.

In a matter of weeks he is up to two or more.

Soon it's bloody syringes in the trash along with the glassine bags.

Now junkies all—me on the pipe, Blue on the needle, and Emerald going back and forth between—we crawl along toward a bland Christmas season in the dimmer light of grayer dawns. And along with the nip in the late November air come colder, harder times. Blue turns up dope-sick on the odd days. He and Emerald start having sudden, bickering fights. They carry on right in front of me, oblivious of my presence, Emerald ranting, crying, and smoldering her way through them, Blue mostly pleading, wanting nothing more in the end than to wend his way back into her good graces. Little by little Blue descends into brooding, sullen silence. Then Emerald begins to disappear for greater lengths of time, saddling me with Blue's inert form for hours at a time, and more and more, when she returns, it's with a story instead of cash or goodies. I continue to cling to a pretense of graciousness, never demanding, but fully resenting that there's less and less in it for me.

At the end of November they appear on Friday night and instead of crawling homeward as usual when dawn comes sneaking up, they both fall asleep in their chairs. Saturday afternoon they leave, but show up again after midnight. Sunday it's the same thing. By the time I figure out that they must be ducking their landlord, they're already settled in, crashing late each night on the bed I have set up behind a partition in the back of the office and disappearing before nine each morning.

When I approach Blue, he bristles at the suggestion that they might be having problems coming up with rent money. Doped up as he is, he still has his pride. But Emerald readily owns up to it and prevails upon our friendship.

"The fucking landlord," she says. "That asshole. I should be straight in a couple of days."

Only I know that by now things have gotten too deep for any of us to wade to shore. What follows is a mad run of crack and dope and strangers in the night. As the word travels to certain corners of Hell's Kitchen that a hit or two for the house might buy you entree, the party that Emerald and I had begun for two—quickly expanding to three—evolves into something of an all-night open house. I find myself playing host to succeeding generations of friends of friends, armed with fewer and fewer social skills, and coming up the stairs with less and less benign intent. And in the comings and goings, the piping up and crashing down, even Emerald reaches the end of her charm. She is all impatient, demanding bitchiness. There is no such word as *no*.

I had been a fatalist up until then.

I was prepared to go down with the ship.

To ride the run to whatever dismal end.

But then, during the haunting hours of that particularly tense and empty night, after two days when there is not a crumb of the stuff to be had for love or money, it occurs to me for the first time— in the forced clarity of that sober interval—that I have come full circle. Twelve years ago, feeling trapped and boxed in, I was relieved to have been "released" to the freedom of the streets. And now here I am, trapped and boxed in all over again.

That really, really pissed me off.

And Emerald and Blue are the closest targets at hand.

The explosion comes a few days later, in the middle of the night, when I stand up, throw open the office door, and demand they both leave at once.

"That's it," I holler, standing by the door. "No more parties, no more smoking, no more ringing my bell. No more."

Blue takes the news gravely but with some degree of equanimity. My guess is he isn't ever completely comfortable with imposing on others. Emerald is another matter. She has, I realize, little tolerance for defiance. I have to face up to the selfish, crack-thirsty, unappreciative, low-life son of a bitch that I am being before—Blue tagging obediently along behind her—she finally storms out the door in a huff.

It would be nice to report that it ended right there. That I put down the pipe for good then and there and leaped into the fullness of life. But it doesn't quite work that way. I still had a wall to crash into before I really got ready to do a one-eighty. That took me another six months. And then, with help, I had to spend another year and a half scraping twelve years' worth of crack residue from my brains.

That wasn't the last of Emerald and Blue either.

A week or so after my scorched-earth rampage, Emerald comes to the door, rings my buzzer, and chirps her name into the intercom as if nothing at all has changed.

"I thought I explained that we're not doing this anymore," I tell her through the speaker.

"I just want to use the bathroom," she tells me, as if I don't know full well that a bathroom is a poor man's crack house.

"Bathroom's out of order," I tell her, as if I think she won't know it's a lie.

"I got something for you," she purrs back, a hint of the old Emerald seeping through.

"Sorry," I say, remembering that first touch of her forefinger on the heel of my palm. "But we're not doing this anymore."

But she isn't taking no for an answer.

Twenty minutes later she has bluffed her way into the building somehow and is pounding on the office door. It's the side of Emerald I don't care for. The part that insists, no matter what.

"You can stand out there and bang all night," I tell her, meaning every word. "But I'm not going to open this door."

There are a few seconds of silence.

But she has to give it one...last...try.

"Please?" she says in a voice so small it hardly makes it through the door.

It's a cruel moment ignoring Emerald's last, sad mew. You can't blame her for playing the cards she has been dealt. It is, after all, the way of the world to yield gladly to women as divinely made as she is, to demand they be all charm. I suppose beauty is as real a burden as anything else. But nothing of any worth would come from my opening up that door.

The next morning, before I even have a chance to go for coffee, the buzzer sounds and it's Bob with a six-pack. We have a history of mad carousal that goes back twenty years. When I let him in, I see the violent red lipstick scrawl on the opposite side of the door.

ASSHOLE! it says, in angry, flamboyant script.

"It must have been some party," Bob says.

"Emerald," I tell him. "She had a little difficulty comprehending the concept of *persona non grata*."

"You threw her out?" Bob asks, incredulous—and sorry he missed the scene. "Wow, that *really* must have been some party."

Bob lives on beer.

And he lives for bars.

I am envious that he is able to stay afloat.

"You know," he says, "the other afternoon, when she was here and you ran out to the store? I was watching her. She was sitting in that chair over there smoking crack. She had on some cheap, tacky thing she must have picked up for ten dollars somewhere, and I'm looking at her and it looks *fabulous* on her. So I say, 'Tell me, Emerald, how come you aren't a movie star by now?' She looks up at me, takes another hit on her stem, blows out this huge cloud of smoke, and says, 'Movie star? Why the fuck would I wanna be a movie star?'"

He laughs out loud at this, snaps the tab off a can of Bud, tilts his head back, and sucks down a good, thirsty mouthful.

"That," he says, "told me everything I needed to know about Emerald."

The next day there is yet another buzz.

It's Blue.

"Can I come up and get my sweater?" he wants to know. "I left it here the other night."

Blue has been a man of his word with me. I buzz him in and go down the hall to the top of the stairs. Through the gap between landings I can see he's not alone.

"Blue?" I call down to him.

"It's me," he calls up.

"And the she-devil from hell," says Emerald, trailing behind him, beguiling as ever.

A Loft on Ninth Avenue. 3:45 a.m. I am so high I can hardly sit still. I am in a place that does not belong to me. The person I am getting high with is a stranger. And we have just run out of drugs. We have been smoking crack in a frantic, compulsive blur. The shock this presents to our systems has rendered our nerves raw and jangled. We move in sudden, jerky motions.

The stranger, not quite as big as me, but younger and quicker, is standing about eight feet away, fumbling through his pockets. I am standing in front of a low couch that is pressed against the wall. He has been rummaging through his empty pockets—between pulls on his crack pipe—ever since he came through the door.

"Damn!" he swears, as if it has finally dawned on him that there is nothing to be found within them. "I'm buggin'."

I can't keep my attention focused on him. My eyes keep falling to the floor. Something in my drug-dazed brain keeps telling me that I am going to find something I want down there.

I'm bugging.

"I need more money, man," I hear him say. It is only with great effort that I am able to pry my eyes from their floor-bound fascination and take a glimpse at him. There is a knife in his hand, the serrated kind, a steak knife.

"No," he says, a darker tone creeping into his voice. "I mean, I need more money." I stand stock-still, my already hyped awareness peaking to new levels. He is a completely different person from the one who came in the door. His eyes have gone wild, the muscles in his jaw jut from either side of his face, his chest heaves.

"Sit down," he says, holding the knife in front of him, motioning with it. He is serious. Desperate. But I am frozen, every limb in my body has gone rigid with coke-perked hyperfear.

"I said SIT DOWN!" he screams. The violence with which he shouts this causes me to flinch slightly. But I know that if I sit down it's all over. He'll ransack the place and do God knows what to me. I cannot sit down. I am afraid of what will happen if I do.

"Okay, okay," I tell him. "I'll give you money." I do not have any. But I tell him this anyway, stepping over to him as casually as I can, reaching into my pocket and pulling out a crackling wad of paper. He falls for the ruse, lowering his eyes to the wad for just an instant, and I'm on him. I lock both of my hands on the hand holding the knife. He yanks, pulls, pounds on my back with his free hand. I'm oblivious. All my strength is concentrated in my fingers, wrenching his wrist, keeping the blade away from me.

Suddenly the handle snaps and the tables are turned. Now I am holding the blade and he is holding on to me. It is clear I am stronger than he is. All I have to do is wiggle out from his grasp long enough to stick him and it will be as good as over.

Only I don't do it. Sticking him will mean blood all over the place, and the place isn't mine. It will mean police and explanations and neighbors peeking in the door. It will mean gossip and rumor for the owner of the place. It will mean he will never trust me again.

The other thing is that I have never stabbed anyone before and, angry and frightened though I am, I can't bring myself to do it. It's a line I do not want to cross. I just want him out.

But he's a real asshole. Doesn't have the sense to give up. "Look, no damage has been done yet," I tell him as we swing each other around, seeking traction on the carpetless wooden floor. "I don't want to have to stick you. Let go and you can split."

—Nothing.

He's beyond reason. Committed to badass. For the next ten minutes we waltz around the room locked in a frantic embrace, careening into walls, knocking over lamps, upturning chairs. As long as I refuse to stick him, he hangs on. Nor can I let him go. If I do, he might pick up something to fight me with and I'll have to stick him.

I manage to muscle him over to the door. But the damn thing opens inward. Every time I get it open, he swings us around and we back into it, slamming it closed again. It's maddening. I can see us doing this for hours. He may not be as strong as me, but he seems tireless. On the third try at the door I spot the intercom.

"All right! That's it!" I shout, panting now. "I don't care. I'm going to buzz Security!" I shoulder him against the door, back to the intercom, and press the *Door* button. The sound of the lock buzzing drifts up the stairs. It does the trick. His body sags.

"Okay, okay," he pants, "put the knife down and I'll leave."

I tell him, "Uh-uh. I'm not puttin' this down until you're on the other side of that door." He won't agree to this deal. But when I get the door open, he lets me push him through it into the hallway. I slam the door behind him and hear him pound down the stairs and out of the building.

I am still trembling half an hour later as I straighten up the loft. I am amazed and relieved that I am not dead or lying bleeding on the floor. When I peer out the window onto Ninth Avenue, I see there is still a trickle of activity along the street. I am wondering where I can hustle up some more money and get another hit.

13

It's time for my nightly crawl. I gather fifty copies of *Street News* into a shoulder bag, head for the subway, and finding the shuttle train waiting for me when I hit the Times Square station, I hustle down the stairs to beat the closing doors.

I walk through all three cars to the back of the train before I do my thing. I can usually spot undercover cops. The giveaway is that they have to drape their torsos with extra clothing to cover all the gear they wear on their belts. They also work in pairs. Spot two bulky mopes pretending to be oblivious to everything and it's as good as seeing a badge.

The MTA has banned guys like me from the subways. We are a bane to their ridership. They'd like to purge all homeless people from their underground turf. And we *Street News* vendors present an all-too obvious target. They have demanded that we cease and desist, and have ordered transit police to seize and arrest us. After being arrested a half-dozen times, I finally got the message and developed an outdoor spot to sell my papers. It's not as good as the subway, though. And the coast seems clear enough for me to do a little business en route.

"Hi, folks," I say from the center of the car. "I thought perhaps some of you might enjoy something interesting to read. So I brought along a few copies of this."

Four years of peddling the paper has taught me a few things. I don't say "*Street News*" right away. I just hold it up. I want them to see the cover story. To find out if that interests them. I know that once I say "*Street News*," it's no longer about what I have to sell. It's about charity. Not that people mind a little charity. But when you petition them expressly on behalf of your own need, they tend to find it presumptuous.

"It sells for only a buck," I go on. "And if any of you would like a copy, please know that I'd be very happy to serve you."

Nothing.

Not even a curious glance.

Sometimes it's like this.

But I know what to do.

"Now, now," I continue cheerfully. "There's no need to push and shove. I have plenty to go around. Please form an orderly line."

The humor nets me a few awkward chuckles and two sales.

Better than nothing.

I go into the next car.

At the sight of me the passengers know what's up. I can sense them bracing themselves for my bother. But nothing ventured, nothing gained....

I do my pitch and it falls flat.

I do the funny bit and it falls even flatter.

By now the train has pulled into Grand Central and as the people file out, a bespectacled lady pauses in front of me, ruefully shaking her head.

"Can't they see you're trying to help yourself?" she laments of her fellow passengers.

"Hey," I say, "they don't owe it to me to buy a paper. After all, do you buy a vacuum cleaner to clean your house, or do you buy it because the salesman needs to pay off his mortgage?"

"But what's a lousy dollar," she insists, "if it will help the homeless? I always buy a copy when I can. I just don't have any cash on me tonight."

"Here you go," I tell her brightly, handing over a copy. "With my compliments."

"Oh, I couldn't do that. You can *sell* that," she says with mild alarm. "You keep it and get a dollar for it."

This gets me slightly ticked.

"I may be on the street," I tell her. "But if I couldn't give something to someone every now and then, wouldn't that make me even poorer than I am?"

But the point is perhaps too abstract.

She just stands there knitting her brow.

"Please," I say, all kinds of things riding on it now, "allow me to give you this."

Her face suddenly brightens.

"Wait a minute," she says.

She sets her purse down on the seat and, digging frantically through it, manages to come up with ninety-seven cents.

"There you go," she says, smiling in triumph.

But it's her victory alone.

I give her a paper and thank her. She disappears into the next car, pauses briefly, and goes out through the center doors. Already the train is filling with passengers for the return trip. I'm putting the change away when I hear the *bing-bong* that signals the closing doors.

I figure I'll do one more round-trip then head for the No. 6 Uptown. I step into the next car, giving it a quick survey for cops, when I see the copy of *Street News* lying on the seat, just inside the center doors, where the lady has left it for me.

Sometimes it's like this, too.

I wear an official *Street News* ID badge when I work. It doesn't carry any legal weight. It's meant to connote that we vendors are involved in a legitimate enterprise. But the premise of *Street News*— helping the homeless—presents people with a more compelling reason to buy the paper than to read it. And an entirely different thought process goes into that decision. One that, in unfortunate contradiction to the badge, positions the seller as a ward of the buyer. It's a conundrum that, try as I may, I can't seem to find my way around.

At the end of the round-trip I have five dollars and change in my pocket. I leave the shuttle and transfer to the No. 6 train. When *Street News* first came out, this was one of the best trains for selling papers. I could get on at Grand Central with a hundred papers during the rush hour, ride down to City Hall and back, and most of the papers would be gone.

That was back when Wall Street was really pumping and the train would be full of stockbrokers. Those guys really got off on seeing a guy hustle. The very smell of enterprise gave them a hard-on. To them we *Street News* vendors were a reassuring sight, living ratification of the humanity to be found in brisk commerce.

These days, although Wall Street is pumping again, the mood is different. Standing up and reeling off a speech is not the attention-getter it once was. Most people have become used to the drill. And weary of it to boot. Now we only remind them of a problem that they wish to turn the corner on and be done with. We are in the very unsalesmanlike business of defying popular demand.

The first car of the Uptown 6 is crowded and noisy. And it doesn't abate when I start my spiel. But I go through with it anyway. Persistence, they say, overcomes resistance. When I'm finished, a guy at the end of the car who could not have heard a word waves me over. He gives me a dollar but refuses the paper.

I can't even push it on him.

This is no boon to my spirits. But a dollar is a dollar.

I get off the 6 at Eighty-sixth Street and head for my spot. As always, the evening streets buzz with money on the hoof. During the Roaring Eighties, a ten-block mélange of bars, clubs, and late-night restaurants was forged out of this once-sleepy residential area. It is now unofficially known as the strip. And every night it plays host to a festive, monied, often boisterous crowd, hell-bent on pursuing a little after-dark diversion. It's work hard and play hard all the way for these folks. Earn it by day, blow it off by night.

The hustlers have followed the money up here. Streetwalkers ply the turf along Second and Third avenues within a four-block radius of Eighty-sixth Street. Ad hoc pot dealers loiter along Eighty-seventh, midway between Lex and Third. And from Eighty-fourth to Ninety-fourth, a rogue's gallery of panhandlers work the constantly moving horde.

You see them shaking their cups outside overjammed watering holes, hovering in front of busy restaurants and fast-food franchises, and working the doors at bank cash machines. Some are solemn, perched silently on the ground with a cardboard sign, or rooted in one spot, methodically shaking a cup. Some press a song or a dance on you, ambling along at your side, daring you to blow them off without so much as a dime. Others imagine themselves host of the ball, yanking open taxi and limo doors as they slide up to the curb, welcoming you out for the night, reciting the pleasures that await you.

It makes for an interesting study in forced coexistence. Even the weekend warriors who descend on the strip from out of town every Friday night seem to regard the hustling homeless as part of the landscape—live slice-of-life displays in a hodgepodge urban theme park. Their "spare some change?" incantations and the chime of coins ringing in their cups are part of the street's discordant music.

Meanwhile those street people who lack the guile to coax a fair buck from the passing trade subsist on petty crime, breaking into cars, peddling the loot cut-rate to the guys in the Korean stores; doctoring the coin returns on pay phones, coming back later to collect the money jammed up in them; riffling the pockets of passed-out drunks, yelling "Are you all right?" as they commit their cool larceny.

The blue-and-whites keep a constant, rolling vigil, scooping up the drunk, deranged, and dangerous. Or idle in front of the madhouse joints, intervening solemnly when the volatile combination of alcohol and testosterone begins to combust.

The hustle on the strip is fed by the action just north of Ninety-sixth Street. Those who've scared up their cop money fly to Spanish Harlem—where crack comes packaged in as little as two-dollar, one-hit vials—then do their dirty in doorways and cubbyholes, their disembodied faces flaring tangerine in the sudden glow of their igniting stems. Then twitch off the high away from the lighted places, keeping their misery tucked into the shadows.

I work just on the periphery of it all.

In front of the Love Pharmacy on the southwest corner of Eighty-fourth and Third. The large apartment buildings that loom over this intersection feed me a regular trickle of customers from the neighborhood. And the strip feeds me a constant stream of fresh through-traffic.

There isn't time enough, as they walk by, for a proper sales pitch. I play off of the spare-changers down the block.

"We don't shake a cup. We sell *Street News*," I chant in counterpoint to their bother. "Latest issue, just one buck."

The people who work inside the Love store have been friendly to me. They often step out and buy a copy. They wish me luck and good night when they lock up for the evening. Sometimes they throw me a pack of cigarettes.

A couple of doors down there's a trendy quick-cut hair salon. Ladies wander in plain and curious, and stride out bold, assured, and freshly coifed. They wink at me as they pass. The gay hairdresser sometimes comes to buy in a gush. He does everything in a gush, it seems. Even the Chinese from the restaurant down the block will sometimes come nodding over.

They all buoy my spirits.

Make me feel like a celebrity.

"We don't shake a cup..."

A guy wearing about half a grand's worth of leather on his back makes his way across the street, a sleek, slender, and blond fox riding his arm. He knows he's got the world by the balls. You can see it in his walk. He pops a crooked grin on his face as he nears, figures to have a laugh here.

"Hey, dude," he says, already amused with himself. "I'm a little short, can you spare some change?"

But he's not ready for me.

I reach in my pocket and come up with a dollar for him. It's cheap, really. Visibility for a buck.

"There you go," I say brightly.

"Hey, man, I was only kidding," he tells me, red-faced now in front of his girl. Just wanted to see what I'd do. Pegged me for a panhandler and thought he'd have some fun.

But the buck is his.

I insist.

I won't take it back.

He can only live with this for five steps down the block, turns on his heels, ambles back up to me, and slides a ten into my palm.

Now *he* insists.

Won't take it back.

"Okay," I say. "You win." I know when I've been outdone. Both he and his girl beaming now. He reels her back in against his hip. A big shot once again.

"*Street News!*"

"Latest issue!"

"Only a dollar!"

A little later I break to make a beer run—get a sixteen-ounce at the deli down the block. I down it quickly in the shadows. My customers would not approve. I betray them in taking pleasure as a fruit of their patronage.

The beer takes the edge off the monotony. Puts me in mellow harmony with the moment. No rush. The money will come. It's a fine night. A perfect, breezeless seventy degrees. People are out having a good time. Walking their dogs, chatting with their neighbors, closing the details of deals on the corner, dashing in and out of taxis, dipping in and out of the joints, zipping by on skateboards, on bicycles, on roller blades, laughing, singing, shouting to the sky. The people who know me say hi as they pass. Throw me a little wave. A few stop to talk.

—Want to know how the paper's doing.

—Want to know how I'm doing.

—Want to know how the Mets are doing.

On nights like this, selling *Street News* is as good as any other grind. There's life in the mix. I'm thinking maybe I won't go uptown tonight. Maybe I'll go back to the office early, nurse a forty-ounce in front of the TV. I don't have to go crazy every night.

I see one of my regulars approaching in his trademark charcoal chalk-stripe-and-burgundy tie. He is with his son, a typical antsy toddler, in a too-large baseball cap, ambling along beside him.

"How're you doing?" he asks.

"I'm doing great!" I tell him.

He looks down at his son and puts a buck in the kid's hand.

The kid's face lights up.

Daddy's being generous.

But it's not what the kid thinks.

"Give the man the dollar," Daddy says.

But the kid is just like any other kid. He likes the feel of his very own crisp buck in his hand.

"C'mon, honey, give the man the dollar," Daddy coaxes.

The kid peers up at me, betraying just a hint of contempt. I don't blame him. I'd happily slip him five bucks not to look at me that way. But his father has a purpose in mind. He reaches down, slides the dollar from Junior's tiny fingers, and hands it over to me.

"Now take the paper," Daddy tells him.

The boy reaches for it sheepishly.

"Remember what I told you?" Daddy says.

The kid shakes his head, "Yes," resigned to the coming bit of drudgery.

"What is the man doing?" Daddy prompts.

"He's selling papers," the boy intones.

"And why is he selling papers?" Daddy wants to know.

"So he won't be homeless anymore," the kid replies, and buries his face in the cloth of Daddy's trousers.

"Very good," Daddy says, civics lesson over. Off they go down the street.

I count my money.

Twenty-three dollars and change.

That'll have to be enough, I tell myself, and step off with a robust, purposeful stride. The man doesn't really deserve my resentment. He was only trying to do The Right Thing. Nor would it do any good to tell him that I am no longer completely homeless. That I work for the paper and sleep in the office. That I imagine myself a writer of sorts. Contrary to its stated mission, there are things that selling *Street News* cannot deliver. That part is an inside job.

But I don't know this yet. I fly along the pavement, voices and faces blurring by, like the walls of a tunnel, as I hurry on, counting off the remaining blocks, clutching the stem in my pocket, not stopping until I've reached the spot I'm looking for, just a few blocks north of Ninety-sixth Street.

14

Sure, life on the street has its drudgery and suffering. But it's a testament to the resiliency of the spirit that even amid the bitter realities of hand-to-mouth existence, one can find refuge in a well-developed sense of humor. (Ha, ha, you're homeless.)

My first inkling of this came twenty years ago, before I ever ended up on the street. I had rented my first Manhattan apartment on the Lower East Side, just a few blocks shy of the Bowery (then known as Skid Row).

There I got to know my first homeless person.

Every morning, without fail, he could be found standing at the Second Avenue subway entrance, wrapped in his wrinkled army jacket, large shopping bag at his feet crammed with sheets of his poetry.

"Spare a quarter for an out-of-work poet?" he would implore the rush-hour passersby.

A quarter got you a photocopied sample of his verses. As I recall, he wasn't likely to have a Pulitzer in his future. But in deference to his tenacity, I often hit him off with some change.

Around this time I got into a dispute with my landlord. It was his contention that I was obliged to pay him his rent, whereas I insisted on reserving the money for recreational purposes. Unfortunately Housing Court sided with him. I got booted from the building and ended up sharing a rent-controlled apartment on the Upper West Side with my business partner.

A few years later I had an early appointment downtown and to my surprise, there at his usual post was the street poet, hawking his dismal rhymes. Only this time it was:

"Can you spare a *dollar* for an out-of-work poet?"

He remembered me immediately.

"What's up?" I asked, riffling through my pockets for a spare buck. "You only used to ask for quarters."

"Sure," he said without batting an eye, "but I'm writing much better stuff now."

Over time my reluctance to adopt the proper attitude toward rental arrangements took its toll. I eventually found myself "non-domiciled." It was during this period—while summering, as it were, in Central Park, and wintering in Grand Central Terminal—that I, like my poet friend, found myself relying on wit to blunt the stings of living life under reduced circumstances.

Of course, I wasn't about to abandon my well-advanced devotion to the great party of life, misfortunes notwithstanding. I was therefore delighted to discover I could underwrite my nocturnal wanderings by virtue of New York's bottle law. This environmentalist-inspired statute stipulates that stores selling carbonated beverages must collect a nickel deposit on every can or bottle sold and must forfeit the same for every empty you bring them.

I doubt, however, if any of the lawmakers were aware of how resourceful homeless people can be. Or that they ever anticipated the deluge of can-laden souls that would descend upon the city's supermarkets as a result of their legislative engineering.

To give you an idea of the stakes, it was reported that even a year after the law went into effect, something like $40 million in deposits remained uncollected by consumers, who found it too burdensome to haul back their empties for the sake of a lousy five cents.

This wasn't lost on the bottlers, however. They reaped a huge windfall from this ecological caprice. And they had no problem with counting nickels. They soon put pressure on the retailers, who in turn made it harder—through ever-increasing rules and limitations—for nonshoppers to redeem large numbers of cans.

So, despite the law's clear mandate that stores accept, without benefit of prior notification, up to 240 cans per person per day, it wasn't long before all but a handful of huge supermarkets declared themselves off-limits to professional canners. Thus, while it was no problem for me to collect forty to fifty dollars' worth of cans in a day, redeeming them quickly became a major hassle.

I remember spending an entire Sunday attempting, in vain, to cash in twenty dollars' worth I had collected the previous day, a quest that took me from Chinatown to Queens and finally to the Bronx. At every stop I encountered either a line around the block, mechanical failure, or some other problem. At my last stop, fistfights broke out, and the store manager shut the whole thing down.

I had to jump the turnstile to ride back to Manhattan and stash my load for the night. On the train I ran into an acquaintance, who asked me where I'd been all day.

"Well, this is the Lord's Day," I told him. "I spent it in search of redemption."

The homeless aren't the only street people. Cops are, too, in a sense. The ones who burn out are those who think it's their mission to eradicate "bad guys" clean off the face of the earth. The ones who make it to retirement reasonably intact are those who accept, often with a sense of humor, that being a good guy is, after all, just another grind.

In New York City it is illegal to spit, smoke, or carry a lit cigarette in the subways. The Transit Authority takes an equally dim view of people riding without paying or those using the subways as a rent-free sales place. To discourage such behavior, they deploy a number of undercover cops.

I encountered one of these guys one afternoon not long after I finally gave up the can business in favor of what was to be a far more lucrative enterprise.

Street News was a brand-new publication then—the first newspaper designed to be sold by homeless people. Before I managed to work my way up to the position of editor, I was one of their top-grossing salespeople. The secret to this success was that instead of hawking the paper one customer at a time on the street, I pitched to a hundred a pop, going from car to car on the subway trains.

The difference in sales made it worth the risk. The papers practically flew out of my hands. The trick was to load up on as many papers as possible before setting out.

This particular day I went for broke and invested every cent I had in papers. Once I got to the subway station, I realized I hadn't allowed for carfare. I was standing by the turnstiles, puffing a cigarette, contemplating my dilemma, when I heard the train coming.

I decided to go for it. I snatched up my bundle of papers and, with a little sleight of hand to make it appear as if I was dropping a token in the slot, I squeezed edgewise through the turnstiles.

But before I could make it to the train, a muscular guy in a plaid shirt popped in front of me. He took in the smoldering cigarette, the ready-for-sale papers, the half-cranked turnstile, and flipped his badge in my face.

"You might as well spit too," he said.

I couldn't help but laugh.

But when he brought out the cuffs, his was the only grin that remained.

"Turn around," he said, "and place your hands behind your back."

I couldn't have picked a worse time to try for a free ride. Up until then I would have been charged with "fare evasion"—a violation—and issued a summons on the spot, not unlike a parking ticket.

But as I was to learn later, TA police had changed strategy. Under the new policy you got charged with "theft of services"—a class-B misdemeanor—arrested, taken to the precinct, printed, photographed, and booked.

If you could verify your ID and address—which few homeless people can—they'd run a warrant check on you and, if you were clean, release you with a desk-appearance ticket, obliging you to come to criminal court at a later date.

In my case, the police had great difficulty accepting the Central Park band shell as a legitimate address. So I wound up spending two and a half days in Central Booking, subsisting on the occasional bologna sandwich and sleeping on a bare concrete floor along with hundreds of pimps, dealers, muggers, and other entrepreneurs caught operating beyond legal sanction.

There are fewer amenities in these holding cells than in the jails to which you are committed if found guilty. The place is designed to break your spirit, to soften you up for the plea bargaining by which the lion's share of cases are resolved.

By the time I got to talk to my court-appointed lawyer, I had recouped. In the intervening time, I had pinpointed the flaw as a result of which, I imagined, I would be completely exonerated.

"Listen," I said when he sat down. "I've been charged with theft of services, right? He gave me a nod. "But the arresting officer apprehended me before I could get on the train! I never got to ride anywhere. In effect I never received the services I was accused of stealing. We gotta move for dismissal!"

I had seen enough episodes of *L.A.Law* to be genuinely pleased with the brilliance of my argument. But when I had finished, my lawyer just sat there, staring at me with such profound sadness, I thought he would break into tears.

"Look," he finally said. "Do you want to get out of here?"

At the arraignment it was determined that my brief captivity in Central Booking constituted sufficient penance for my egregious rip-off of a $1.25 ride that I could now be safely released back into decent society. The irony of the whole thing was that before they let me go, I was handed a standard voucher form to sign that, when taken to an office on the third floor, entitled me to receive one free New York City subway token.

What a concept!

What else could I do but laugh?

What keeps running through my mind, during the daily drill of using this town's awesome mass transit system, is that it is *our* subway. I sometimes forget this, thinking of it as *the city's* subway. But every New Yorker is a shareholder in the hundreds of trains, miles of track, dozens of stations, and army of workers that comprise what is about the biggest transit system anywhere. And seeing it from that perspective, I sometimes feel the kind of pride that, say, a co-op apartment owner feels in having a piece of a major building.

The MTA has tried exhaustively to instill this feeling of oneness with the subways. But they are undercut by a number of factors.

Their name for one thing.

You cannot easily bond with something as monolithic as an "authority." Something like "The Metro Group" might be less forbidding, or "Friends in Transit." I suppose neither one would look all that impressive on a business card.

The fact that the transit system exists at all is a testament to an earlier New York, which had the awesome optimism and fearlessness to embark on gargantuan projects decades in the making. New Yorkers then were possessed of an irrepressible spirit that distinguished us from any other compilation of brick and mortar that dared call itself a city. It was what drove us, and the fact that we have tried to make this city more things to more people than could ever be comfortably or easily achieved never stopped us from trying.

These days there are fewer Manhattanites struggling in the trenches (though it seems the trenches themselves are deeper), so routine accommodation of urban life's little inconveniences is unfortunately being bred out of us. More of us are seeking to thrive these days, where once it was the struggle to survive itself that made us great.

And there has been a corresponding and much-publicized flight, among those with alternatives, out of the subways, away from the urban swell, and often out to the suburbs, where things are a tad less heterogeneous. This has led to a growing conviction that in suburbanizing Manhattan, these expatriates can be drawn back to the fold.

I say let them go.

They have a right to their expectations, and all the better that there are places that can deliver on them. But it is as fruitless to try to install in New York City the more casual comforts of, say, Larchmont, as it would be to attempt to transport the vitality and diversity of this town to the sticks.

Pointless, too.

Places like Larchmont already exist.

Naturally, the flight of upper-middle-class New Yorkers will erode the city's tax base and all that. But their stake in our public and social institutions has been steadfastly diminishing anyway. More and more, they send their kids to private schools, hire their own security forces, go to private-sector hospitals, even hire their own street-maintenance crews in some areas. They can hop in a cab and go—door to door—wherever they want without having to hobnob with anyone they don't want to. They don't really need our institutions.

But the rest of us do.

So the logical thing to do is to waste less tax money competing with the private sector for those upscale dollars and to put more of it to work serving those of us who, day by day, actually depend on public amenities.

Our schools.

Our hospitals.

Our subways.

Sure, there may be less to go around for a while. But it will have been better spent. And if it means we have to struggle to make do with less, so be it.

We're New Yorkers.

We're used to it.

15

In 1993 I created a fictional persona called Homey, who inhabited the back pages of *Street News*. Homey was the quintessential street person, and he responded to reader's questions about the streets and the people who lived on them. What I liked about the column was that, of all my writing, it came the closest to engaging readers in a dialogue. Every Homey letter in the mail felt like a gift.

A few excerpts...

We got a loaded envelope this week from Shephathiah Gordon of Manhattan: one writer, three questions. I decided to tackle them—one at a time—in the order they were asked.

Dear Homey,
I have three questions: (1) Where did you get your name?

Dear Shephathiah, I might well ask the same of you. A year or two before this column became a reality, a few of us vendors were kicking around ideas about what we would put in *Street News* if we had the chance. We came up with a Q&A column using the photo of a street person named Carl who purported to have a Ph.D. We were going to call it "Ask Dr. Carl."

The concept was later picked up when I joined the editorial staff and Richard Moskowitz, acting business manager at the time, suggested "Ask Homey" as a title, and the name stuck.

My real name is protected, however, by the State Secrets Act.

(2) What services, if any, does *Street News* provide for its vendors?

There are numerous organizations that help feed, clothe, and counsel street people. *Street News* augments these services with a mission specifically targeted for those with the motivation to go out and provide for themselves, and to do so with minimum trade-off in terms of dignity and self-respect.

It is true what they say about no free lunch. Even well-intentioned handouts cost the recipient a bit of independence or self-esteem. *Street News* provides the do-it-yourself kit, encouragement, and support for those who might not want to wait in line for someone else's help.

(3) So who are you? At least Ann Landers shows us a picture of herself in her columns. But no one knows what you look like or what your credentials are.

Get a life!

Seriously, your humble advice-giver is flattered by your interest. Last things first. I have no qualifications whatsoever (isn't this a great country?) except for the fact that for the last eight years I have lived with less inconvenience than you might imagine on the streets of this city. In exchange for answering readers' questions, *Street News* gives me ten free papers, a box lunch, and occasionally allows me to crash on the couch.

The fact that I do not have a degree on my wall does not imply any opposition on my part toward higher education. Perhaps readers could indeed benefit from a more lettered author.

So I have decided to start the *Send Homey to College* fund drive. I assure you that any money collected will be put to good, scholarly use—such as reeducating myself to apartment living through life experience; discovering uses for an ATM machine other than as a night-light; or finding out what, besides redeeming cans, a supermarket is good for. All worthwhile pursuits, I'm sure you'll agree.

All checks and money orders should be made payable to cash (cash will be gladly accepted as well). Donations are not tax deductible (unless you deduct them before you write the check).

Of course I might lose my authority as a bona fide street person, but it isn't as if I'm getting rich at it anyway.

Dear Homey,
I want to help the homeless people of New York and do whatever I can. The problem is I get mad when I see people asking for help who I know aren't homeless. It makes me not want to give anymore. What can be done about these people?

Helping people and getting rid of con men are, to my mind, separate aspirations. It is not clear to me why your desire to do one should be predicated upon the other.

Like all of our institutions, charity has its hucksters. We encounter stock-market hustlers, cops on the take, bought-and-sold politicians. Should we therefore abandon our desire to increase our fortunes? Maintain order? Govern ourselves?

Human commerce, in whatever form, requires exercising a degree of *caveat emptor.*

But if discerning between the genuine and the fake presents too much drudgery, perhaps instead of trying to help homeless people as a matter of course, you might single out *a* homeless person or family and develop enough of a relationship to determine true need.

Keep in mind that money is not the only means by which you can help people. Isolation, alienation, and disenfranchisement—issues that aren't easily faked—take the greatest toll on people living in the streets. Your genuine interest in getting to know someone cut off from society can be, in and of itself, supremely effective.

Dear Homey,
I was doing a documentary on a homeless man named Brad. After several days of shooting, he has disappeared. I haven't seen him for two months. So the film has become an "in search of..." type thing. How would you suggest I go about locating him? He used to sleep under a theater marquee on Forty-sixth Street. I've enclosed a photo from the documentary.

It just so happens that I know Brad. I met him sitting under the very marquee you describe. I don't know where he is at the moment, but I can venture a few educated guesses. The NYPD are now purging midtown of homeless people as part of their so-called "quality of life" action.

Anything from "aggressive" panhandling (is there such a thing as "passive" panhandling?) to drug possession makes him fair game.

So the first place I would look is Midtown Court, where area quality-of-life charges are prosecuted. You would need to have something other than a photo. The more info, such as date of birth, Social Security number, first and last name, date and time of arrest, and so on, the better. The court clerks are not going to go out of their way to find your missing person. Despite the fact that this court has been bankrolled in part by area private business interests (a fact I find extremely disturbing and of dubious legality), it is still, after all, a part of the city bureaucracy.

You might check city hospitals as well, but there, too, the more details the better.

If push comes to shove, you might have to employ some good old shoe-leather detective work. Get to know other street people in the area and, when the timing is right, bring up the subject of Brad. You might get better results if you keep your camera packed away. It can be intimidating. Ditto for the photo. You might be mistaken for police. Best just to say you knew him and wondered what happened to him. There are few secrets on the streets. Someone out there has info.

Dear Homey,
   I have fought my way back from the streets on my own. I gave up doing drugs and found a steady job and I now have my own apartment.
   The trouble is, I barely make enough to cover expenses and am now in danger of being evicted for back rent. I've applied for Public Assistance, but their programs are all skewed to benefit druggies, psychos, and people with AIDS. There doesn't seem to be anything for people like me who have been responsible enough to turn their lives around but still need help to keep going. I suppose once I do end up back on the street without a job, I'll be eligible for all kinds of benefits. Do you think this is fair?

You are a Republican in the making.

In the words of "quality of life" Mayor Giuliani, "No social program is perfect." Of course, as a candidate he extracted much political mileage out of pointing to the kinds of ironies to which you refer, as indicative of then-Mayor Dinkins's failed leadership.

Now as an insider he, too, has to face the fact that government attempts to engineer society—even his current "take back the streets" incarnation—will always produce a degree of injustice. Politics is, after all, a numbers game, and pro forma solutions are, by their very nature, inhuman.

Yet without some instrument for expressing our collective hopes for society, we seem to be at a loss.

So the government—flawed social mechanism that it is— nonetheless tries to do what it can and, yes, the results are far from satisfactory.

In your case it seems that the Human Resources Administration has narrowed its parameters so as to give worst cases first priority. The old "squeaky wheel gets the grease" approach. This dovetails nicely with the prevailing popular desire to get the most disturbingly, indigent, infected, addicted, cup-shaking, moaning-and-groaning underclass out of everyone's faces. If not for their benefit, then for the sake of everyone else's serenity. It also has the effect, when coupled with a dwindling budget, of squeezing out all but those in the most dire circumstances.

Ergo your chagrin.

Merry Christmas.

Dear Homey,
Why are conditions so bad in the shelter system? Were conditions always so bad? Aren't enough taxes poured into the shelter system?

If you listen to advocates for the homeless, there is not enough money being spent on either affordable housing or the shelter system. If you listen to "reformers," money isn't the answer at all and the shelter system only succeeds in making people wards of the state.

To some degree they are both right.

A fundamental problem is that shelters—intended as a last resort—have been applied as a reflex solution to what is a multifaceted problem. We tend to turn to legislation to enforce that which we desire to be as a people but fail to do on an individual basis. This is an awkward and ultimately unsatisfying way to go about being human to one another.

City-run shelters are a result of Coalition on the Homeless lobbying efforts to enact "shelter on demand" legislation. What we do under threat of legal retribution we tend to do grudgingly, uncreatively, less effectively, and, most important, without quality.

Thus, in city-run shelters criminals hiding from the law, drug addicts needing a place to crash, and other shady types drawn to the underground commingle with those who just plain need a hot meal and a night in off the streets.

The failure of these shelters should teach volumes about the efficacy of compelling people—as opposed to inspiring them—to fulfill what is our natural impulse to take part in the social contract.

It may sound corny to say that in order to make a difference we have to care, but it has been duly demonstrated that if we don't care, nothing we try will quite work.

Dear Homey,
Why are you liberals so reluctant to admit failure? Why do you insist on clinging to your failed policies?

I'll surprise you. I agree with the conservatives' view that liberal policy is badly flawed. I don't agree, however, with their solution, or that their policies will ultimately fare any better. The fact is, all policy is inherently flawed. The resort to policy—particularly right-minded policy—is a concession to human failure. It seeks to install, pro forma, into our legal code what we as humans recognize as proper and necessary but fail to execute by our own moral code.

Therefore the spirit in which policy may be written does not carry through in application.

As long as men are flawed, and as long as we persist in seeking remedy outside ourselves, there will be policy of some sort (though I suggest it should be a matter of last—not first—resort). And as long as there is policy, it will be flawed.

Policy is never the real issue.

The real issue is the hearts of men.

Dear Homey,
I have read where you have said that policy is flawed. Would you agree, then, that affirmative action is flawed because it discriminates against nonminorities?

I also said in that piece that policy isn't the issue. In that regard I am less concerned with your conclusions about affirmative action than I am with the thinking behind them. You overlook the inescapable fact that any action tendered under the social contract requires something from us. That's the whole idea. If I decide, for instance, that it's a proper thing to share my lunch with the next fellow, I certainly have to resign myself to not having it all to myself.

When I was out there picking up cans on the street, people told me the proper thing for me to do was to get a job. And the fact that

I now write this column means that some other poor slob may still be scribbling prose on napkins, though affirmative action had nothing to do with it.

Yes, if there are a finite number of positions available at a given time and a number of them are reserved for minorities, fewer whites will get those positions than otherwise would. And those who labor under the belief that we live in a true meritocracy claim that that kind of thing undermines it. But if this is truly a meritocracy, then the best will rise to the surface and those with less to offer will ultimately sink. Personally I believe that in the ebb and flow of human events, merit shares the bench with a host of other considerations.

Employers are faced with a choice, under affirmative action, between earnestness and expediency. They can address the spirit of the thing in earnest, going the extra mile to recruit minority candidates who meet or exceed the necessary qualifications (and unless you subscribe to the theory that whites are inherently superior, this can be done). Or they can employ the expediency of the numbers game, hiring the requisite skin color for show. As I have said, the issue is never policy, the issue is the hearts of men.

Affirmative action by expediency prompts letters like yours. I propose to put another thought in your head. I ask you to consider the proposition that concepts like affirmative action, while benefiting others, are essentially driven by our desire to elevate ourselves.

*   *   *

I'm sure most Americans take comfort in the fact that racism has been abolished in this country. Not the practice, of course, but as a topic for public discussion. A few years ago Jimmy the Greek overstepped his authority as an ABC Sports commentator by expounding on the nature of slave breeding and the impact it has had upon sports.

"As slaves," he said publicly, "blacks were bred for heavy labor, so they have thicker thighs." He went on to speculate that this gives some blacks a physical competitive advantage over most white athletes. On the heels of these remarks he was roundly chastised by the press, summarily booted off the network, and consigned to bear the mark of a bigot forever.

I couldn't figure out what all the fuss was about, and I'm a sixth-generation black American. What he said was historically true. Black people were at one time bred like horses with particular attention to their ability to perform certain tasks. And as for the ABC executive brain trust that arrived at the conclusion that racism had no place on their network, it's an odds-on bet that they operate in a world where they seldom, if ever, encounter any black peers. Their response was not so much a true denunciation of racism as it was a response to the *appearance* of racism. The object being not to disturb the picture of America as we imagine it to be.

Jimmy, for his part, may have been ham-fisted and somewhat insensitive. He might even be a bigot, for all I know. But though his comment didn't speak at all well of the white, southern, slave-owning aristocracy, search for any disparagement of black people in it and you won't find any. His only sin, it seems, was reminding us that though black and white Americans may now drink from the same trough, for the most part they have arrived there with dramatically different histories. Not at all a bad thing for us to be reminded of, to my way of thinking.

Recently Reverend Herbert Daughtry likewise earned himself a scarlet *R* by proclaiming—at a press conference no less—that Hasidic Jews "seem to have difficulty adjusting within a pluralistic society." He said this during a call for calm following the release of the city's report on the Crown Heights riots after a black child was run down by a car carrying a Hasidic Jew. Naturally, his remarks had anything but a calming effect on the volatile swirl of emotions surrounding the whole affair. And I wonder myself what in God's name was going through his mind when he chose that particular occasion to make such an observation.

But you'd be hard pressed to make an honest case that race baiting was on his agenda. If it was, it was infinitely less blatant than when mayoral candidate Rudolph Giuliani led a delegation of Jews from Crown Heights to the steps of City Hall to accuse then-mayor David Dinkins of offering preferential treatment to blacks. The group had originally approached Giuliani—a former prosecutor—to find out what progress had been made with the criminal investigation into the murder of a Yankel Rosenbaum that occurred during the riots. And though he was perfectly positioned to get some answers, he used them instead as pawns in his polarizing grandstand play.

We all tend, unfortunately, to be suspicious and resentful of what is foreign to our experience. And for sure there is no shortage of high-profile misanthropes these days, who make a nine-to-five of trading on such fears and doubts. And so long as they don't directly upset our sense of denial about racial and ethnic bigotry, they remain unchallenged as they fan the flames of resentment. So instead of saying "the Jews," they refer to "the liberal media elite," and instead of talking about "the blacks," they refer to the "inner city," and so forth, enabling us to bypass any intellectual scrutiny of the prejudices that are churning our emotions. This tactic so "legitimizes" any hidden vitriol that it is often unconsciously and wholeheartedly embraced by those of us who would otherwise repudiate any implication that we harbor bigotry.

Most of us cannot stand bigotry—which is why we recoil at remarks like those made by Jimmy and Daughtry. At bottom, we supremely wish to be done with the whole dilemma and go on about our lives. A fair enough aspiration.

But how to do this?

Do we get farther by denial? When *New York* magazine columnist Joe Klein observed in print that "statistically, most crime is committed by blacks," should he be challenged on the truth of his remark, or for having touched upon the sensitive issue of race?

It seems to me that before we can put bigotry to bed, we must clear away the great confusion about what are the proper parameters for interracial coexistence. And for that to happen, the subject of race itself, ugly, dispiriting, and prone to occasional blunder though it can be, must be taken back out of the closet. The current trend is to dismiss any and all dialogue concerning differing experiences among different racial/ethnic groups as liberal blather.

If Jimmy the Greek, Reverend Daughtry, and Joe Klein are to be cast as symbols of the problem, then it can't be overlooked that the Rudy Giulianis, Rush Limbaughs, and Newt Gingriches of the world, in their constant suborning manipulation and denial of our still-great racial divide, are also the problem.

In knee-jerk furor over anything that does not support our one-nation version of cultural harmony, we are diverted from true vigilance. And we allow the seeds of further intolerance to be sown and a far more bitter future harvest to take root.

It's relatively easy, when writing editorials, to pick a target and start firing away. Or to stand firmly on one side of a hot issue or topic and spout off. But nothing in this imperfect world is beyond dispute.

I'm not saying there is no need for a sense of right and wrong. There is. But people's lives proceed under an infinite variety of circumstances. And I find it perilous to pass judgment.

However appropriate might be one's stance on an issue, it is most often the case that emotions are the tail wagging the dog of reason.

Beneath the "right" and "wrong" of issues and the "pro" and "con" of our positions, however, lies the vital matter of our relationship to the events behind them, and to the people involved in them. So I have always tried to get to the *why*, as it were, beneath the *who, what, where*, and *when* that drives our actions...Anger, resentment, envy, fear, frustration and so forth.

16

Manhattan has only two seasons: shiver and swelter.
Digging ourselves out from a crippling crust of snow, as we did
many times this winter, we long for the bright, balmy days of summer, conveniently forgetting about the *h* word. It's not the heat, as they
say, it's the humidity. But heat, humidity, whatever, it always seems
worse in the city than anywhere else.

That's because it is. There is something called an inversion layer
hovering just above our skyscrapers. It has to do with all the hot air
being propelled out the back end of millions of city air conditioners,
acting together with other atmospheric phenomena and forming a "ceiling" which traps in all the sweaty weather. The worse it gets, the more
air conditioners pop on or notch up, creating the infamous "vicious cycle."

This sets off other v-cycles. When it's hot, New Yorkers get hot
under the collar. What pisses us off the most is being robbed of our
urban cool. Step out of doors on any Manhattan dog day and no matter who or what you are, everything crisp and businesslike about you
soon becomes damp, limp, and clingy.

The ultimate place for this meltdown is underground in the subways, where everything is cranked up yet another notch. Down there it's shiver and swelter all in one place. Because, to be precise, the air conditioners that refrigerate the trains don't actually cool the air. What they do is remove heat—by way of the low evaporation threshold of freon gas—and all that hot air ends up in the tunnels and platforms, turning it all into an underground sauna.

What's truly amazing is that despite the chronic and recurring failures of every other aspect of the transit system, the air-conditioning seems to be the one thing that's just about always working. Station repairs can go wanting for years, service may be killed on whole lines at a time, carloads of commuters can be trapped in tunnels for twenty minutes, but they never, ever kill the chill.

You can't convince me this is a fluke. The Transit Authority is fully aware of what a dangerous proposition it is to cram hundreds of edgy New Yorkers cheek to cheek into a narrow car while the mercury is peaking. Cut off the ice streaming from the vents and you might have such carnage that the Long Island Railroad disaster would seem like a bad-hair day by comparison. It just goes to show you what the MTA is capable of when their very lives depend on it.

Summer is for T-shirts.

And underground they take on particular significance.

Veteran straphangers seldom speak to strangers on the subway. We let our clothes do the talking. We do this sort of thing year-round, and not only on the subway—most often to convey something about status. You might have twenty, thirty grand in the bank, or an eight-hundred-dollar wad riding on your hip, but only you will know it. If you have real money, however, the cut of your suit and your Hermès attaché will discreetly inform all who come near that they are approaching rarefied air.

But most of us are left to jockey for position with status symbols that are woefully entry-level. We can't afford the name-designer power suit, but the designer name itself—emblazoned on a T-shirt—tucks neatly into the declining blue-collar budget.

Once summer has descended and almost everyone, from proletariat to modern-day robber baron, strips down to a T in their more casual moments, the crush of sloganed torsos makes for a riotous, voiceless cacophony on the subway. Scrawled across one man's chest is *DON'T ASK ME 4 SHIT* in bold block letters One glimpse into his eyes and you know he means it.

Brrr.

You're elbowing your way into a packed subway car and suddenly you're staring down the barrel of a .45 printed on the back of some misanthrope's sleeveless muscle shirt, accompanied by a cautionary *BACK OFF!* caption, and you do precisely that. *The air-conditioning is definitely working,* you think to yourself. *There's a serious chill in this car.*

And the miracle of the daily cold war of traveling mass transit is how, when we walk away from it unscathed, we are reinforced somehow. It makes us more of everything we are than if we had kept ourselves isolated altogether from the great underground stewpot of summer in the subway.

There is a sleek silver train with a big gray-and-white *S* for an eye that hustles passengers east and west across Forty-second Street.

In the middle of Brooklyn you have a different kind of shuttle, one that transports a far different crowd than its sister midtown line.

It's the Prospect Park–Franklin Avenue shuttle. And though you may have never heard of it, it has been ferrying straphangers back and forth since the 1800s, long before the more familiar version started making its crosstown runs in the thirties. It may be hard for us to imagine a subway system without these intermediate-route services, but the fact is that neither was part of the system's original plan. Both were pressed into service, ad hoc, as additional routes came on line. And in 1981 the Brooklyn shuttle was shuttered altogether for a time. It turns out that for nearly a century, "not a single dime" had been allocated to upgrading it, according to an MTA spokesperson, leaving it in such disrepair that officials deemed it unsafe. When $60 billion became available for rebuilding the subways, a lot of passengers talked about renovating the Franklin line. But the MTA talked about keeping it permanently closed.

They argued that with only ten thousand daily riders—the lowest in the system—it was a money loser (a cardinal sin in the eighties). But ten thousand people are ten thousand people. And for these ten thousand, typically lower-income passengers, the Franklin shuttle is more essential to them than is the other shuttle to their counterparts in midtown, who enjoy other options. For that reason advocates for the Franklin shuttle riders argued that money should be allocated for capital repairs to structural deterioration and replacement of the antiquated wooden platforms.

Neither side prevailed completely.

The MTA reluctantly shored up the shuttle's crumbling retaining walls and reopened the line. But they stopped short of a full renovation. Talk continues, however—about rebuilding and about shutting down. So, besides hustling people back and forth between the A/C and D/Q lines, the Franklin shuttle also provides a bit of grist for the political mill. Councilwoman Mary Pinkett did a little public grandstanding on its behalf but fell short on follow-through. Mayors Dinkins and Giuliani have together cut a total of $750 million from the city's share of subway-reconstruction funds, which doesn't help. But the bottom line seems to be that, coming from the borough of Brooklyn, the voices of ten thousand subway riders are cries in the wilderness.

My guess is that the Franklin shuttle will go on traversing squeaky track beds to wobbly stations until it is no longer physically viable, and then it will be unceremoniously—and permanently—padlocked.

The image of street people has always been associated with an unnatural devotion to some substance. In the old, skid-row-bum, rail-riding-hobo incarnation, the liquor bottle was an emblem as indispensable as Mulligan stew. But booze-ravaged as these souls were, they made handy naysayers against a complacent, material world. So we tended to afford them a measure of folk-icon deference and allow them a wee bit of turf.

But when street people's substance of choice changed, so did their once-benign image. It's hard to say to what extent the Reagan era and subsequent policies would have altered the homeless picture had there not been a concurrent explosion of crack-cocaine use—though there's little doubt the one had an impact on the other. And there is no denying that, this time around, crack has been a major factor in the cascade of people landing penniless on the streets.

In the mid eighties, when homelessness first emerged as an urgent national crisis, we were prepared to address it in the traditional way, with compassion and human interest, what I call the "sandwiches and sympathy" approach. However, once the crack connection became common knowledge—implying that homeless people might be complicit in their own destitution—a lot of people began to feel they had squandered their compassion on less-than-worthy subjects, and public sentiment soon began to turn.

Today you hear people branded "homeless huggers" with the same contempt once reserved for "nigger lovers." While "legitimate" homeless people might yet be considered "unfortunates" by a lingering few, druggies, particularly those hoveling on city streets, are deemed morally bankrupt "lowlifes" beneath human consideration.

In the ten years I spent on the street, also abusing drugs, I've met just about every type of junkie out there. And I'll tell you this: Though some of them, myself included, might be perfectly capable of immoral acts while using—as would you and nearly anyone—I cannot say of any of them that they were immoral people.

Sure, a druggie may mug you for a fix. A boozer might even kill you in a drunken rage. But this has little to do with their morality. It's a clinically proven fact that psychoactive chemicals, such as alcohol and drugs, actually shut down the brain's moral center. Be it a priest or a child molester, the effect is always the same, to put you beyond the rule of conscience, and it gets progressively worse over time.

Of course no one puts a gun to anyone's head and forces him to indulge in the stuff. And a common assumption is that drinking and drugging are activities moral people eschew by nature and immoral people readily take to. Boozers and druggies routinely concur on this point.

But it is simply not so. The truth of the matter is that so long as an addict believes this is the case, there is little hope for turnaround. Addicts—and I include alcoholics in the term—are absolutists. It's all-or-nothing with them. Indeed, their principal flaw is an inability to cope with a world that refuses to comply with the picture of order or perfection toward which we basically all aspire. For an addict, it's Eden or nothing.

The pathology of an addict is that once he has had a taste of "heaven"—chemically induced or otherwise—he relentlessly mines the source of it for more, determined to maintain the sensation all the time. It is the thing that hooks him because it is a metaphysical impossibility, so that each diminishing return only inspires him to try again all the harder.

Nonaddictive personalities contain the requisite pragmatism to negotiate the inconsistencies of an imperfect world. They possess a capacity for middling convictions, to put it another way. Even in matters of morality. When a nonaddictive personality is harmed—whether physically, psychically, materially, or morally—he seeks closure by settling the matter one way or the other. The addictive personality will demand nothing less than absolute moral justice as he understands it. Since absolutes are ever elusive in this world, these demands pile up unsatisfied.

You may have seen bag ladies or winos walking down the street roaring drunk, screaming at buildings, accusing everyone in sight of all manner of evil and intrigue. These modern-day Don Quixotes represent one striking example of people who may have endured, as have we all, some injustice, real or imagined, but who, unlike most of us, find that injustice unconscionable to accept. Alcohol may have come into play as the salve for their anguish, but since alcohol doesn't do anything to help them deal with the matter, when its effects wear off, the anguish looms even larger, driving them back to drink. From there on, the cycle progresses beyond the bounds of their control.

This is the pattern for addictive personalities whether they are using or not. When they do use—and there are any number of things besides drugs and alcohol that addicts use—the deficit they incur is not moral in nature but spiritual.

This is amply borne out by the fact that twelve-step programs, which are the only treatment universally recognized as effective against all forms of addiction, stress spirituality as the essential element.

The object of AA (Alcoholics Anonymous), NA (Narcotics Anonymous), CA (Cocaine Anonymous), and other step programs is for members to help each other establish a relationship with a higher power (as each is able understand that). Not in order that they achieve moral perfection but so that they might achieve spiritual growth. This is the unique thing an all-or-nothing personality can latch onto that, so long as it is earnestly pursued, offers no prospect of self-destruction. It simply takes all the relentless machinery that creates the addictive personality and sets it on "reverse."

To one degree or another we all want essentially the same things out of life: love, respect, happiness, a sense of fairness and justice, a sense of well-being, a sense of purpose and value, and the feeling of being connected to something substantial, lasting, and secure. And as certain as it is that none of us will get what we perceive to be our rightful share of these things all the time, it is just as certain that we all balk at accepting this fact.

It's called the human condition.

The characteristic of absolute, unwavering devotion to something—common in those whom we might in error consider "lowlifes"—may well be, when directed toward spiritual growth, the essential element we readily assume drunks and druggies are by nature missing.

No, drugs and booze are not the route to paradise. But man's natural inclination toward the spiritual has been taken over by the ubiquitous belief that it is more important to concern himself with material and physical things. And in the increasing busyness and clutter of modern life, it often takes an extreme blow—not unlike the ravages bought on by active addiction—to snap us out of it.

I do not know anyone who considers himself a hardworking, moral, churchgoing, nonaddicted American who would go to the lengths to which recovering addicts and alcoholics go for the sake of spiritual growth.

The urgency is just not there.

So, frightful and miserable as active addiction may be, presuming to scorn the prospects of those caught in its grip is our folly. For the addict is being propelled toward a point of decision that the rest of us find time and reason to avoid indefinitely.

As they say in the rooms of AA, religion is for people who are afraid of going to hell, spirituality is for those who have already been there.

In its May 11th issue, under the unfortunate title "Street News," the *Village Voice* published a report on what would seem to be a rash of homeless people run amok. At the center of the story: Jeffrey Rose, a homeless, mentally ill man who, one night on the Upper East Side, snatched a two-year-old from his mother and began to stab him with a pen. It was a nightmare crime, tailor-made to arouse the kind of bold-faced headlines and hysterical community reaction in evidence throughout the piece.

Early on, the writer suggests that homelessness is at the root of the problem, when he cites it as being at "the top of the list" of modern urban complaints. Yet even the mother of the attacked child disputes this. "There was no purse-snatching or panhandling involved," she was quoted as saying. "He was not interested in me or my money. He wanted to stab my child." *Clearly, then, the imperatives of living on the streets are not the issue.* But to read the *Voice*, you would think they are. The word *homeless* appears no less than fourteen times in the brief article.

The assault was unarguably a crime. But there is only one reference to crime. And at the bottom of the crime, unarguably, lies one man's mental illness. Yet mental illness is mentioned half as often as—and is always attached to—the word *homeless*.

It's ironic that if Jeffrey Rose were a typical homeless person, both child and mother might have been spared their horror. And doubtless the mother would have preferred the relatively benign attentions of a panhandler—or even a purse-snatching for that matter—to a deadly attack on her child.

The *Voice's* carelessness is harmful. For how is she, or her community, to pursue an effective solution when at the outset the problem is misdiagnosed? Already the imprudent skew on the Jeffrey Rose story has incited citizens to anger. And already they are proposing actions that, if they are carried out, are likely to guarantee that the same thing will happen again.

"If they can't guarantee our safety," the East Seventy-seventh Street Block Association proposes, shut down the neighborhood outreach center where Rose occasionally went for referrals. Putting aside the fact that no one can guarantee anyone's safety in this or any other city, what exactly would shutting the facility down accomplish? Mr. Rose's illness has driven him to such attacks and will continue to do so with or without a referral center on the Upper East Side. But sever even this minimal thread to treatment and he and guys like him will be even more prone to psychotic outbursts. *The referral center is not the issue either.*

The convoluted logic inherent in making it the issue is that if there were no center around in the first place, Jeffrey Rose might not have been in that neighborhood and therefore might not have attacked that particular child. Here we get to the crux of what block associations are essentially about. They are about turf. *Close the center*, their logic runs, *and at least those people won't be in our neighborhood*. But however reasonable may be the desire to feel safe around one's home, the turf approach to the problem is, in essence, self-defeating.

The pain, anger, and frustration of this woman whose child was so senselessly abused is real and human and inevitable. But when organizations act in anger, or out of fear and frustration, they become little more than mobs, the group equivalent of Jeffrey Rose. When Seventy-seventh Street Block Association co-chair Marge Sweeny proclaims to "serve notice," that "Jeffrey Rose types will not be tolerated," her voice becomes kin to the one in Rose's misfiring brain that told him a swaddling infant was a threat to be reckoned with.

We all wish nothing more for that mother, her stricken child, and all New Yorkers for that matter, than that their health and security go untroubled. But that can't happen unless the same applies for the health and security of people like Jeffrey Rose as well. This is not "liberal crap," as quoted in the *Voice*. It is practical reality. Jeffrey Rose's lack of health and security is precisely what led to the attack in the first place. *This is the issue*. And if we ignore it, we ignore his victims—past present and future—as well.

Whatever it takes to relieve the plight of street people, it should not be pursued at the expense of other people's well-being. This we understand. But neither should the prerogatives of turf be so blindly and supremely pursued. And during times of crisis, journalists and community leaders have in particular a special responsibility to unwaveringly defer to reason. In our anguish over a city that seems on the verge of crumbling around us, reason tells us that closing ranks only represents that much more fragmentation. Reason cautions that we fail in our impulse to protect our own unless we seek to protect us all.

17

His name is Marvin. He's twelve years old. He lives in a Brooklyn project. He's "strapped" with a nine-millimeter. And he's out "to get a body on it." Chances are the first excuse he gets, he'll blow someone away with the thing. Not for the sake of larceny necessarily. Not even for the sake of crime. But to buy himself some leverage. He knows, as do most of the kids in the hood his age, that if he establishes a rep for being tough, the bad guys will cut him some slack.

So he is primed to kill.

For the sake of perception.

If this scares you, take heart. There's a new governor in Albany and he has made it clear that he intends to be the new sheriff in town as well. In fact, George Pataki's election relied, in great part, on his ability to establish a rep for being tough.

"As governor of New York State," said he, "I will bring back the death penalty."

Unless Pataki is a complete idiot—and even among politicians *complete* idiots are rare—he knows that the death penalty has a negligible impact on the rate of crime. This has been exhaustively demonstrated. On the other hand, just what is effective in the war against crime remains a matter of hot debate.

But Pataki also knows, as does every other give-'em-the-chair posturer, that dealing out death to the bad guys is an idea that resonates with a frustrated, edgy populace. So in making this campaign promise his first priority, Governor Pataki, like Marvin, has signaled his willingness to kill—for the sake of perception.

Neither he nor Marvin is very willing to entertain any arguments as to the futility of their positions. The only difference between them, then, is that Marvin is up-front about what he's doing and why, nasty as the whole business is, and that he's willing to pull the trigger himself.

They are ordinary working New Yorkers who leave behind the familiar surroundings of home each weekday morning for the increasingly alien turf of midtown, to toil—behind cash registers, in offices, in elevators—at making a living. It is safe to bet that most have had it with the daily gauntlet of hustlers, druggies, and dealers who boldly ply Eighth Avenue from below Forty-second Street all the way up to Fiftieth.

And as wave after wave of rush-hour police sweeps hit the area, they take consolation in this highly visible evidence that something is finally being done to clean up the streets. So when a Tactical Narcotics Team (TNT) springs from an unmarked van on Eighth Avenue early one evening and snatches up a dealer and his customer, they are heroes in the eyes of these ordinary working New Yorkers.

But then one of the cops decides to body-slam his quarry against the van a few times, though the guy had thrown up his hands in surrender as soon as the police appeared. Then, after manhandling the cuffed prisoner around to the front of the van, he repeatedly crushes his head into the windshield.

I spot a few druggies looking on mutely, cowed—by having narrowly escaped a similar fate—into silence. A few peep-show shills look on with vague interest. They have seen this before. And truth be told, I let my own outrage over the gratuitous violence percolate in silence. But to my left a man in a gray suit, briefcase in hand, obviously no friend of the street drug culture, calls out.

"Hey! Hey!" He hollers angrily. "Is that necessary?"

Then another voice rings out.

"You've got witnesses here," says a man who, in his manner and dress, could have been the first one's twin.

The crowd of spectators gets behind these two then, and getting the message, the cop finally lets up. Maybe the two who spoke up believe that the prisoner who got roughed up is the scum of the earth, symbolic of all that is wrong with this city. Yet in that defining moment, when he was being pointlessly brutalized, they knew how much was riding on what was happening to him. So they rose to his defense.

Ordinary working stiffs, en route to dinner and the tube. But in their world-class sensibilities, their inclination toward the best in themselves, truly great people. The hope of the free world, for my money.

It's easy reading, nine typewritten pages (one side). It has a heavyweight paper cover and, on it, the lengthy but promising title "REFORMING NEW YORK CITY'S RESPONSE TO HOMELESSNESS *City of New York Department of Homeless Services.* " Below the title the date, October 1, 1993, is neatly typed.

But what, exactly, is it?

"It's our philosophy for what we are going to do about the homeless," sings Sam Szurek, media director for the newly formed DHS, which, according to the hype, is going to streamline, economize, and otherwise revolutionize the city's response to the homeless.

Going to seems to be the operative phrase here, though, along with *will make*; *in the process of,* and other "Tomorrow is another day" action phrases. The booklet is woefully shy on specifics such as timetables, cost projections, and a number of other such revolutionizing details.

Take eligibility requirements, for example. Under the new order of things, "There will be requirements to determine the eligibility of prospective clients," Szurek explained to me over the phone. Urged to be a tad more specific, he added, "If you're on the street with no sustainable alternative, you're eligible."

Ah, that explains it.

The release of this nonbook might seem politically motivated to Dinkins watchers. But Szurek hastened to assure me this was not the case. "We don't get into politics," said he. "We have a job to do. And we're going to do it no matter who's in office."

"Who established the department and hired its staff?" I wanted to know.

"Well, the mayor did," he says.

Between mayoral wannabe Giuliani's position papers on what he "intends" to do about the homeless (lock up the squeegee guys), and Dinkins's end-of-term masterpiece of DHS "is gonnaism," it would appear that a whole lot of paper shufflers are hard at work on the homeless problem.

In theory, that is.

18

If, at the time of this writing, you should ven-
ture to Times Square and wander down the south side of Forty-second Street toward where it intersects with Eighth Avenue, you'll get
a parting glimpse at a New York tradition.

I call it God's corner.

That little patch of pavement—on the pedestrian side of the chain-
link fence encasing the corner parking lot—where Billy Sundays have
been plying the Lord's word since as far back as I can remember.

I first discovered The Deuce as a preteen. Artie—a buddy from
the Bronx—and I played hooky there, slumming around in search of
some genuine diversion.

In those days West Forty-second was an all-sideshow concrete
circus. Tourists and natives alike flocked there to get a gander at the
macabre wonders procured for our amusement by cigar-chomping,
wrinkled-suited, sidewalk impresarios. It was the very seediness of these
hard-edged yeggs that led us to imagine how supremely visceral would
be the fruits of their efforts. When they prevailed upon us passersby
not to be shy, but to "step right up" for "only a thin dime," most

agreed—Artie and myself included—that for an honest look at the oddities they so vehemently shilled, ten cents was indeed a bargain.

Artie and I ducked into one gritty shock parlor after another that afternoon, finding gratification for our adolescent fascinations in about half of them. We felt cheated when we finally peered through the little "porthole" in the belly of Hubert's Museum to discover— after an interminable wait on line—that "the world's tiniest living mermaid" was in fact a normal-sized woman done up in mermaid drag and reduced to inches by some obvious trick of mirrors.

A few doors down from there was a freak show under the *Ripley's Believe It or Not* banner. There we saw the bogus *Petrified Giant* and the all-too-real two-headed calf. The sight of that tiny mute, doe-like creature lying before the gawking crowd on a bed of old mottled straw has stayed with me all these years. A second, dead head had been grafted crudely onto the side of its little neck, all for our perverse entertainment. And—flippant youth though I was—standing there gazing into that calf's pained little bovine eyes, I couldn't help but feel obscene and diabolical.

Making our way down the block, Artie and I were the targets of every front-door barker. But the most passionate voice, out of this din, came from a stalwart soul, near Eighth Avenue, literally standing on a soapbox and stumping for Jesus. The presence of this man, and the thought that God's emissary would stalk the unrepentant into such a smoldering pit as The Deuce, put me in touch with fears far worse than any horror chambers into which Artie and I were unquietly venturing.

Years later, on the threshold of adulthood, I returned to The Deuce to find that its attractions had been reduced by one dimension. Gone were the grim dungeons I remembered. And in their place were more than a dozen shimmering, winking movie marquees stretching down the block. I whiled away countless hours munching popcorn in front of those giant, flickering screens, swept up in the gruesome devices of shock cinema. Some days I would race from one theater, as soon as the lights came up, right into another, from horror movie to splatter flick to blaxploitation film.

Afterward I would find the subway in the gathering dusk, hobgoblins and serial killers lurking in the shadows of my mind. If it was Saturday evening, I would hurry past Rosie the midget preacher, who held court by the parking lot, wailing into the night about the wages of sin. In the midst of all the divertissements along The Deuce, this little sawed-off woman was a draw. She always had them standing four or five deep. Down the subway stairs I would hasten, Rosie's fire burning my ears, knowing the train would not take me far enough.

Over time the screens on The Deuce got smaller as the all-night movie houses were one by one replaced with glittering triple-X fantasy palaces, each one a maze of one-man theaters so small, there was hardly room enough for shame.

Compared to the previous attractions on the block, porno held no particular appeal for me. But one day I ducked into one of the booths for a quick blast on my stem. And the instant that cocaine rush went quivering through my brain, I became mesmerized by the sexual antics shimmering across the little screen. Flicking through the endless channels, feeding more quarters into the slot, compulsively smoking and reloading my pipe, and feeling paranoid about opening the door, I found myself stuck inside the booth for what seemed like hours, until everything but my lust had been consumed. I emerged from this lunacy and scurried down The Deuce feeling as transparent as Saran Wrap, convinced, in my buzzed-out brain, that all the people I passed on the street were clucking their tongues at me.

It seemed fitting, then, that even God's corner seemed to be aflame with anger, and that the acerbic Black Israelites holding forth there had come not necessarily to assure our place among the chosen but to proclaim the certainty of theirs.

Perhaps it's equally appropriate now that a more calculated brand of redemption has come to Times Square—now that most of the sex shops have been shuttered, and the novelty stores have been nailed shut, and The Deuce seems bound toward more homogenized pleasures—that God's corner should now play host to bespectacled, new-age moonies, Magic Marker in hand, quietly diagramming the Lord's purpose, on a portable flip chart.

And I, too, have stopped groping for the dark and outré, reaching for the light of spirit instead of the glow of the pipe. And when I dawdle along The Deuce these days, even as I wonder at the scale of the new, gaily stuttering lights of its superstores and megastores, the absence of any spirit at all in this, the heart of our great city, cuts me to the quick. Without souls at risk, The Deuce seems to have nothing left at stake but venture capital. It appears that even God himself has abandoned his corner and made off for some other dark region of this city where, good, bad, lost, found, or in-between, beat the raw, true hearts of men.

In writing Grand Central Winter, *I didn't want to do the obvious thing— make it a recovery story. It was the stuff in the middle, more than the before and after, that interested me. But it has since been suggested by the publishers of this edition that an afterword touching upon the recovery thing might be interesting. And I couldn't resist the opportunity to tell a story.*

—*L.S.*

Project Renewal, Lower East Side, May 1996

In a head-to-head with one of the counselors here—a stout, almond-skinned woman who takes herself and her job very seriously—I am asked what kind of job prospects I see myself having at the end of my treatment.

"Why, I'm a writer," I tell her with cocktail-hour casualness. "I have a contract to write a book."

"Yes, yes," she said, "but it will certainly take you time to finish this book. How are you going to make a living in the meantime?"

"Well, as I said, I'm a writer," I repeat. "I'm not completely without contacts. There's more than a good chance I can land a column or something. Maybe not at the *Times*, but something."

She leans forward in her chair, in deference to the gravity of her next question.

"But what if it turns out that for some reason you can't write?" she asks.

"I don't—I'm not sure what you mean," I stutter, panic rising.

"I mean," she says, "what if you have to do something else for a living?"

Mind you, it was barely four weeks earlier that I had joined the three hundred–odd other lost souls, blown in here upon one desperate wind or another. In the depths of a dismal, spiritless night, me and a smoking buddy of mine, whom we'll call Irish—both of us well into separate binges fueled by ill-gotten gains—had recited to each other the time-honored pledge of drunks and druggies alike. "This is it," we told ourselves. "We've had enough. We are sick and tired of being sick and tired. We are going straight, once and for all. . . ."

Only, with both of us holding, and me with a pocketful of cash, we decided it'd be best to first purge ourselves of all temptation with one last big blowout. Of course, both of us being longtime veterans of the pipe, Irish and me were way past the party days. The psyche can, after all, only take so much hypersensation. Somewhere along the line your circuits simply short out. After that, all you ever get for your blast is raw, angry nerves, a queasy dread bubbling in your gut, and a frightening sense of vulnerability down your spine.

Five minutes after booking ourselves into a fleabag hotel room, firing up our pipes, and getting that first rush, the two of us were quivering with crack paranoia, me huddled by the window peering out through the edge of the shade like a cornered B-movie gangster, and Irish cowering at the door, trembling and sweaty, his eye glued to the peephole. Whatever we imagined out there coming to get us wasn't going to take us by surprise.

We spent the better part of the next six hours locked in this grim ritual. No sooner did one rush subside than we were back sucking on our stems again for another lunatic dose. At the end of it we emerged—stumbling, bleary-eyed, and ragged—into the late-morning light. Slouching along the streets, headed for who knows where, I happened to glimpse our reflections in a store window. We both had the same defeated look on our faces. A look that said *I don't want to do this anymore*. It didn't take much of a nudge after that.

"Look," the counselor says, her eyes drilling into mine, the need being to peer beyond whatever words I might say, to glimpse, if she can, into the depths of my soul. "Were you writing while you were active?"

"Yes."

"And what did you do with the money?"

"I-I bought drugs."

"Right," she says, pulling the string on the trap she has set. "So now what happens when you leave here and go right back to that same lifestyle?"

I have only myself to blame for walking into that one. I know the drill by now. This recovery thing has not been the hand-holding business I assumed it would be. There's no such thing as getting comfortable, no such thing as coasting along, no such thing as having it your way. Since getting high is all about instant gratification, appeasing anything other than an earnest desire to get clean and sober is considered counterproductive. You have only to reveal an inkling of wanting something and they promptly throw obstacles in your path.

This is what defeated Irish. They had promised him right off he'd be allowed a call home—ostensibly to let his family know he was all right, although what he really wanted to use the call for was to get some money sent to him. But the counselors kept putting him off and putting him off, stringing him along for a good two weeks, and the next thing I knew he was out the door in a huff, his clothes in a plastic bag slung over his shoulder.

Seeing the set of his jaw as he stormed out, I had no doubt he'd be back getting high in no time. And although I knew good and well this would only buy him more pain and madness, a shudder of envy passed through me thinking of him out there and me still in here. I even toyed with the idea of cutting out myself but was stopped by the most unlikely thing—my ego. If I walked out, I'd admit to everyone there that I couldn't cut it, that I had failed the program. And I was just too needy of other people's esteem to do this.

It had never been suggested to me, however, that writing might be a casualty of my recovery—until now. And realizing that I have been clinging to the idea of finishing *Grand Central Winter* the way a shipwrecked man clings to a reef, I sit there, gaping back at the counselor, the unasked question *Am I willing to give up everything familiar to me for the sake of my recovery?* hanging in the air between us, me hating the very thought of it and at the same time knowing—from the endless rounds of lectures I've already sat through, from all the Hazelden videos we've been obliged to watch, and all the recovery literature they have put in our hands—that the questions you hate most are precisely the ones you have to tackle.

Of course, I am expected to answer, "Yes, I am willing to go to any lengths for the sake of my recovery." Those are the openers in this business of getting and staying clean. But it has also been impressed upon me that only rigorous honesty will serve this purpose well.

It will do me no good to simply tell this woman what she wants to hear.

"If I can't write, I can't write," I finally say with more confidence than I actually feel. But to my surprise I discover, at the same time, that I actually do mean what I am saying, that that's how much I do not want to fail the program.

There's no reading how the counselor takes this. She just settles back in her chair and plods on down the bill of particulars she must ask me, by means of which I presume she is able, by some unfathomable code, to sort out the true state of my recovery despite whatever obfuscation or denial I might throw her way. When it is over, she utters a *thank you* designed to convey nothing more than that she is done with me.

As I leave her office, a rush of what we've learned to call "consequential thinking" kicks in. I begin to mull over the legal trouble not finishing the book could bring me, since the advance money I was fronted had long ago gone up in smoke. I shudder at the thought of having to face all the naysayers who doubted my having the stuff to produce a book in the first place. I chew on the wholly unappetizing prospect of being released back into the world not as the budding author I imagined myself to be but as just another reformed crackhead starting from zero all over again.

But then I recall the words of Mr. Jones from half a lifetime ago, back when I peddled vacuum cleaners door to door for a not-so-reputable firm, up and down Gun Hill Road in the Bronx. (Mr. Jones was, of course, the husband of Mrs. Jones—the ubiquitous salesman's name for all female prospects—whom I had managed to enamor of the $500 machine I was hawking.) At issue was the snaky sales contract, which not only exacted a usurious annual percentage rate for buying on time but was configured so as to oblige you to pay interest on the interest itself.

Try as he did, Mr. Jones just couldn't reconcile why this should be. And, desperate to fill my quota, I pushed every button I could to close the deal, even going so far as to suggest the need for solidarity between two brothers of color.

He was a young man, and he carried himself with quiet serenity—never rising to anger in the face of my dogged persistence, never becoming flustered by my abstruse arguments—and after a good twenty minutes or so of back-and-forth with me, he finally sighed, still not at all satisfied he wasn't being taken for a ride, and picked up the pen.

"Well," he said, signing the contract with an offhand shrug, "I'll still have to get up and go to work tomorrow regardless."

Later, during a cigarette break, me and my fellow partners in recovery mutely puff away in the yard behind the treatment facility, each of us contemplating the distance yet to go before we can truly declare ourselves free of our addictions. Still haunted by Ms. Counselor's unwelcome prognostications, the simple grace of Mr. Jones's words works like a salve on my psyche, releasing me from the tyranny of expectation. I begin to feel the most peaceful, Zen-like satisfaction blossoming in each moment that passes. And then I am giddy with it, realizing, in one swooping rush, that this is precisely the feeling we were all really groping for every time we reached for the pipe.

Half a dozen months from now I will be well into the outpatient phase of my treatment. I will have found—through the happy discovery that it is not a necessary condition of my recovery that I give up writing—that few things come back to be so completely yours as the ones you are willing to let go of. And, in the midst of all this, my new counselor, a recovered alcoholic who has been through the Twelve Steps and thereby reached a "spiritual awakening," will impart to me another memorable gem.

"The door to Hell always locks from the inside," he'll say.

And I will know exactly what he means.

But right now, taking a page from Mr. Jones's book, I allow myself a mental shrug.

"Whatever the day may bring," I tell myself.

And it is like waking from the dead.

Grand Central Winter

Lee Stringer

ABOUT THIS GUIDE

The suggested questions are intended to help your
reading group find new and interesting angles
and topics for discussion for Lee Stringer's
Grand Central Winter: Stories from the Street. We
hope that these ideas will enrich your conversation
and increase your enjoyment of the book.

Many fine books from Washington Square Press
feature Reading Group Guides. For a complete listing,
or to read the Guides on-line, visit
http://www.simonsays.com/reading/guides

DISCUSSION QUESTIONS

1. Lee Stringer has said, "I wanted to put flesh and bones on what they call the issue of homelessness, but not write about it as an issue. I wanted a book about the '80s, when a lot of people were feeling a deepening sense of despair, not just the poor." How does *Grand Central Winter* achieve these goals?

2. Instead of simply telling readers about life on the street, Stringer shows readers life on the street. What techniques does he use to do this?

3. What is the style, or the voice, in which Lee Stringer writes each of the pieces in *Grand Central Winter*? Do you find his perspective realistic or stylized? Angry or dispassionate? Sentimental or clear-eyed? Explain.

4. Describe the nature of Stringer's politics, particularly in light of the "Dear Homey" letters in Chapter 15.

5. Alongside the expected images of violence and squalor—images which wholly dominate media depictions of homelessness—*Grand Central Winter* breaks refreshing new ground by also putting individual faces on the denizens of the street, and by observing various acts of kindness, humor, and even heroism. How did this book challenge your preconceptions about homeless people? How did it alter or reinforce any of your convictions about social policy and reform?

6. Stringer has been driven by a pair of powerful addictions—to crack cocaine, and to writing. How are these twin obsessions linked, and how do they shape and color the odyssey of *Grand Central Winter*?

7. Beginning with the preface, the book characterizes the 1980s as a time of extreme economic disparity as well as racial and social estrangement. *Grand Central Winter* digs beneath the surface of the storied Reagan era to reveal how the other half of America lived at the time. How do you look at the 1980s now, and what was your own experience during that decade?

8. "In New York City," writes Stringer, "there are three centers for people living on the street: Central Park, Grand Central Terminal, and Central Booking." In what ways have Stringer's portraits of these settings—in addition to Hell's Kitchen, Times Square, and the Upper East and West Sides—changed your conceptions of New York City? How does Stringer's New York compare to Woody Allen's New York? To Spike Lee's?

9. Which story in Stringer's memoir affected or surprised you the most? Why?

Q. I imagine the reactions to this book have been very strong. On your book tour and in readers' letters, what are some of the more interesting opinions and perspectives you've encountered?

A. Most people are surprised at the readability—a frequent comment being that they couldn't put the book down. It doesn't necessarily occur to people that the subject matter will engage them in quite the way it does. Or that, being non-homeless, there would be all that much for them to relate to. I suppose the expectation was that this would be the kind of book that good conscience might urge upon you, but that you'd be in for something bleak and dispiriting. But what I found interesting about my experience is that most people living on the street do not exist in a constant state of despair, and that except for their circumstance, they deal with the same issues we all do, and that they have stories—above and beyond that they find themselves materially threadbare—as worthy of telling as anybody else's. *Grand Central Winter* does the work of a novel in this respect even though it is a memoir. You start with your characters wanting something, and this propels them along on a personal journey at the end of which they are to some extent transformed. The most gratifying response I've had from readers is that they pick up on the spiritual undertone running throughout the book. They pick up on it almost by osmosis because I believe I only actually mention the subject once in the book.

Q. Was there a particular piece of advice that was inspirational to you during the process of writing *Grand Central Winter*?

A. Well, of course I quote, in the foreword, my once editor Janet Allon-Wickenhaver's advice that I stick to telling stories, and the Nelson Algren quote about writers being at their best when they don't know what they are doing—perhaps I should explain what that means to me:

There is the kind of writing done by those who have developed craft enough to master the writing process—who can pretty much preset in their mind what the book is going to be about and where it is going to go—and who can by and large manage to get that all on the page—I certainly did not have that kind of deftness at my immediate disposal. Then there is the kind of writer who every time he sits down wonders how on earth will he fill up the blank page and has to just churn away until he comes up with something worth reading—unable to master the process, he has to surrender to it. That's more me, than the other thing.

I found two interesting things about this approach. One, it demands honesty as a best policy—since making stuff up convincingly requires an enormous amount of craft—and honesty, if you can get to it, has a certain resonance with a reader. Two, when you give yourself over to the process it becomes a kind of journey of discovery—one in which the reader gets to take the trip with you because, not knowing where you're going, you're not tempted to plow a path directly there. This makes for much meat on the bones.

The third piece of advice—guidance really—came from a good friend and fellow writer by the name of Peter Blauner. I went through a tremendous amount of angst and doubt and fear while doing the book and Peter made it clear to me that these were not aberrations, but actually a part of the writing process—a very valuable part of the process in fact. This was an enormous help to me. I don't think I would have finished the book without that bit of insight.

Q. Have you stayed in contact with Emerald, Blue, Suzy, Richard, and the other figures in the book? Have they read *Grand Central Winter*?

A. I ran into Emerald and Blue after I had finished the manuscript, but before the book was published, and have not seen either since. But my suspicion is that they both have found a way to read it—though perhaps not by shelling out twenty bucks for a copy. I'm sure they have other, more urgent priorities on which to spend their money.

Richard has read the book and I have visited him, Suzy and the kids since it's been published. They have had a second child, another girl, in the intervening time. Suzy has become all the more reclusive and refused to come out of the bedroom, so I didn't get a chance to ask her if she read it. I rather doubt it, but who knows. My longtime friend Bob I see all the time and while the work was in progress I let him read an excerpt from the chapter involving my brother. He was in tears when he handed it back to me. Since then he has urged that my next work be *Bob, The Book*.

Q. What advice would you give to aspiring writers?

A. That's easy. Write. The main thing that transformed Lee Stringer from aspiring writer to actual writer is the years spent with my butt in the chair and my fingers on the keyboard. Write and love writing. Because when you get down to it, every finished book represents hundreds—even thousands—of days and nights not doing other life things. So I should say write—and get your stuff out there, even if you have to give it away at first (and you'll do better, in this regard, if writing is about being heard rather than about earning a living) but get it out there as often as possible and learn to frame a proper and constructive context in which to benefit from the feedback you get.

Q. And what would you say to those interested in supporting social programs for the homeless?

A. You know—and I'm sure this will be more answer than you bargained for—the current conventional wisdom is that six decades of social tinkering has left my race worse off than ever, or that it has at least introduced a whole round of new, perhaps more subtle, but equally oppressive ills. I agree with this in many respects—although not necessarily out of the same, tidy rationale conservatives are so fond of putting forward. So I am not a big fan of social programs. To me they represent an attempt at excercising humanity by remote control.

Helping others is a tricky business, while the desire to do so might be quite natural, we cannot assume we are all naturally good at it. People often ask me, for instance, "How do I know if I give a homeless person money it won't be used for the wrong thing?" Well, if your impulse is to avoid being taken, it seems to me that you're probably not going to be all that fluent in the business of giving.

In a way, the first person to help in all this is yourself; to bring yourself into the right grace and spiritual light to help others. There's a lot more listening and waiting to it than there is overt action. Good intentions are not a license to intrude on the next fellow with wholesale presumptions about where they should or shouldn't be at any given point.

Most social programs are too result-oriented to even touch this sort of thing. In order to maintain their mandate or funding they must herd their clients toward a certain predetermined outcome, so that they have evidence that they are doing the job. What this overlooks is that it is never promised that in our good-doing we always get to see the fruit of our efforts—certainly not on schedule with our expectations. We don't always get to witness the miracle. And I don't know of any social institutions—outside of those involved in pure medical research—that have the serenity to accept this.

Having said all this, I will add that there are plenty of people around to whom all this comes naturally. There are givers in this world for sure. And fortunately, some of them actually end up working for social programs. Now, if you discover a social program deploying several of these precious souls, that would be your best bet because when you get right down to it helping others is pretty much a people thing.

Q. When can we look forward to reading another Lee Stringer book? Will it be another memoir?

A. Kurt Vonnegut once said to me, "You know Lee, you don't *have* to do another book. You've shown us you can do it. You don't have anything to prove. You're not obliged to anyone." It made me think. I mean I just *assumed* I'd do another book. It was the obvious thing to do. And I think what Kurt was saying is that you need mare reason than that.

So I thought about it and realized—hell yeah! This is what I want to do. This is what I am about. And have since been at work on another memoir kind of thing—a pre-homeless one. I've also been invited to be part of five or six anthologies due out next year.

And speaking of Kurt, we have a nifty little book together entitled *Like Shaking Hands with God* which should be out concurrent with the publication of this paperback. It was crafted from a number of public and private conversations we have had between us on the subject of writing. I've read the galleys and the great thing is it's not just a transcript, it's a real book. I also have it in my mind to do a novel, but we will have to see how that process works out.